If you're ready to consider why your relationship with God may be in a holding pattern, this book is just what you want. *The helpful insights Dr. Carlson offers are biblical and hopeful,* with honest illustrations from his own journey and the journey of others. *You will find needed guidance to grow closer to God,* no matter where you are in your journey.

—KLAUS ISSLER, professor of Christian Education
and Theology, Talbot School of Theology,
author of *Wasting Time with God:
A Christian Spirituality of Friendship with God*

Everyone I know wishes spiritual maturity was as microwavable as macaroni and cheese. It's not. It comes one step at a time. Dwight Carlson marks the steps from the wisdom of Scripture and the wellspring of life. *This book will bring light for many who feel stuck in the darkness.*

—JOHN ORTBERG, teaching pastor,
Menlo Presbyterian Church
author, *The Life You've Always Wanted*

This engaging and comprehensive discussion of stages on the journey of spiritual transformation should *be well received by all who take their own journey seriously* and especially by those who accompany others on theirs. Frequent references to the author's own life make it clear that the book does not result from library research, but from living life on the journey of Christ-following. *I recommend it to all who long for fullness of life in Christ.*

—DAVID G. BENNER, PH.D., C. Psych.,
Distinguished Professor of Psychology and Christianity,
Psychological Studies Institute (Atlanta); director,
Institute for Psychospiritual Health (Toronto);
author, *Sacred Companions, Surrender to Love,
The Gift of Being Yourself,* and *Desiring God's Will*

Dwight Carlson has written a book with which every Christian will be able to identify. Every follower of Christ has been in one or more of the stages of growth that he describes. *Carlson is strong in emphasizing the need for Christians to continue growing and maturing in the faith,* and he identifies the important role that other people play in our progress towards maturity in Christ. He ably discusses tensions between faith and works, and the danger of following one truth to the exclusion of others. Ultimately, *he sees the transformed life as one that is focused wholly on Christ, rather than on one's own obedience to religious expectations.* That kind of Christ-centered faith, expressed through love, will produce obedience to the will and work of God in one's life. This is an accessible book, written for a lay audience, and it will certainly be helpful to many.

—GLENN R. PALMBERG,
president, The Evangelical Covenant Church

Overcoming the 7 Obstacles to Spiritual Growth

Dwight Carlson

HARVEST HOUSE PUBLISHERS

EUGENE, OREGON

Cover by Koechel Peterson & Associates, Inc., Minneapolis, Minnesota

OVERCOMING THE 7 OBSTACLES TO SPIRITUAL GROWTH
Copyright © 2006 by Dwight L. Carlson
Published by Harvest House Publishers
Eugene, Oregon 97402
www.harvesthousepublishers.com

Library of Congress Cataloging-in-Publication Data
Carlson, Dwight L.
Overcoming the 7 obstacles to spiritual growth / Dwight L. Carlson.
p. cm.
Includes bibliographical references.
ISBN-13: 978-0-7369-1766-7 (pbk.)
ISBN-10: 0-7369-1766-7
1. Christian life. I. Title: Overcoming the seven obstacles to spiritual growth. II. Title.
BV4501.3.C367 2006
248.4—dc22   2005025436

Printed in the United States of America

06 07 08 09 10 11 /DP-KB/ 10 9 8 7 6 5 4 3 2 1

Dedicated to
Dallas Willard & George Samuel,
models of Christlikeness for me.

Acknowledgments

I want to thank each person who has given me permission to share his or her story. I am also grateful to a number of friends who have been kind enough to read this manuscript and to make many helpful suggestions. I am reluctant to start naming them as it involves so many, including men in three different Bible-study groups. You know who you are and I am deeply indebted to each of you.

However, I must mention Ed Lassiter, a fellow companion on the journey who has encouraged me from the outset of this project, has read four versions of the manuscript, and has made many valuable suggestions.

Thanks also to my daughter, Susan Carlson Wood, for editing and helpful comments.

And last but not least, to my dear wife, Betty, for her continual support and help in rewriting many sections.

Finally, I want to thank Terry Glaspey, Barbara Gordon, and the entire Harvest House staff for their patience and assistance in several revisions of this manuscript.

Contents

Preface

This book is about an authentic relationship with Christ. It is not about the trappings of Christianity, but the *person* of Christ and experiencing his life. It is the result of my lifelong pursuit of God—a journey that has had its ups and downs, starts and stops. I have hit my share of obstacles along the way. It has only been in more recent years that some of the more important truths have penetrated my awareness. So I share from my life, and others' as well, to illustrate the steps to maturity in Christ, to how Christ can be our very life!

My prayer is that God will use this book to move you to a fuller comprehension and experience in living the joyous life of faith, basking in God's love, that you may become acutely aware that Christ is literally dwelling in you. May these pages foster your growth into the *manifest presence of Christ*—a Christ-intoxicated life.

To get the most out of this book, I encourage you to read a chapter a week and meet with a friend or small group to discuss its contents. There are questions at the end of each chapter to facilitate discussion, along with suggestions for assimilating its truths into your life the following week. After chapters 1 through 7, you will find some questions to help you evaluate whether or not you might be stuck on your spiritual journey.

Unless otherwise noted, biblical texts are from the *New American Standard Version.* I have used other translations as indicated, when they more vividly portray the meaning of the text and the point being made.

Part One

Seven Obstacles to Spiritual Growth

We all hit obstacles on our spiritual journey and get stalled (or, more frankly, stuck) from time to time. For some it is a flat tire that quickly gets fixed, and they are on their way again. Others blow an engine or get into an accident and go off the road and end up in a deep ditch—tougher obstacles to deal with. Sometimes we don't even know we are stuck. In this first section we will look at some of the more common ways obstacles obstruct our spiritual pilgrimage.

Stalled on the Journey

With the incredible growth in attendance in many of our churches and the great influence Christians are having in certain spheres of society, why is the divorce rate among Christians as high as in the secular world?[1] Why do teenage Christians engage in premarital sex as often as those "in the world"?[2] Why is it that so many dedicated Christians are grinding out a dutiful existence and showing so little evidence of victorious living? Where is the peace, joy, and contentment that Christ spoke about? Why do so many feel the institutional church is irrelevant to their lives?[3]

Christian pollster George Barna says, "One of the greatest challenges facing any ministry, no matter what its form is...[how do you define] success." He goes on to say: "And we've got to break the [current] mold...which says that success is about church attendance, and church budgets, and church programs, and church staff, and square footage and buildings....Jesus didn't die for any of that stuff. He died to see people's lives completely transformed."[4]

Running church better is not the answer. Working harder at what we are doing won't cut it. Something must be missing... something *is* missing. But what?

After many years of counseling patients and being in positions of Christian leadership, I've concluded that millions of Christians have hit obstacles and gotten stalled or outright stuck on their spiritual journeys. Sometimes whole churches get stuck. Many are oblivious to the fact, and those who are aware often don't know how to get any traction. Many are dedicated, hardworking, weary Christians with their façades firmly in place. Maybe you will recognize yourself—or someone you know—in one of the following examples.

Stories from the Stalled

Harold[5] is a structural engineer and a dedicated, gung-ho Christian who knows his Bible. He is a faithful elder at church and leads a Bible study at work, as well as a small group in his home. Harold is best known for his black-and-white answers to complex problems and his strong opinions about most things, especially religious and political issues. Harold religiously tithes. Recently he lost a fair amount of money on some stock, and now he struggles with whether he can "rightfully" subtract ten percent of the loss from his tithe. Harold has no idea he is stuck in "believe right theology."

Jake is a draftsman in the same company that employs Harold and is convinced that every believer must "contend for the faith." His colleagues peg Jake as contentious, whereas his wife, Ann, is the most gracious, giving person anyone could imagine. Not surprisingly, she has suffered from severe depression most of their married life and has needed professional help. She describes the counseling as "very helpful." Nevertheless, she will probably stop the therapy soon because Jake continually badgers her saying, "If you'd just trust Jesus and obey the Scriptures you wouldn't need counseling."

A fellow in their company wants to join the weekly Bible study that Jake and Harold lead. However, since the newcomer is a fairly strong Christian and doesn't believe in "eternal security," Jake doesn't want him to attend. He fears that he will adversely influence some younger Christians in the group. Jake is unaware that he has taken on the role of being an "Expert Christian."

Sheryl certainly doesn't have a problem such as Jake's or Harold's. Once legalistic and quite dogmatic, she experienced a wonderful transformation brought about by the Holy Spirit, who led her to the truth of living in God's grace. Gifted as a teacher and vibrant in her faith, Sheryl's Bible class eventually drew more than 100 women. She discovered that she didn't have to work to earn God's love because "his grace covered it all." Gradually this thinking resulted in her discarding all rules in the Christian life and implying that *everyone* will be saved because "God's love is unconditional." Sheryl is stuck as a "Grace-Abuser."

Pastor Bill grew up in a midwestern town. With his charismatic personality he excelled in everything he did. He was a dedicated Christian, attended Bible school, had a beautiful wife and two delightful little daughters. All seemed to be going well as his congregation grew from 150 to over 400 in three years. But pastor Bill enjoyed the nicer things in life: fine cars, a large home to "host his parishioners," and "sabbaticals for study" in beautiful islands and exotic places. Attendance plateaued about the same time that his deacons noticed that he wouldn't look them in the eye when they spoke with him. Unexplainable items were charged to his expense account, and money was missing from the benevolence fund. He left his first church, and in the ensuing 20 years he has had a number of small congregations and ministries. Questions about conduct seem to litter his pilgrimage. He now has a new wife and a grown daughter who won't speak to him. A number of fine people have tried to talk to him over the years, but he blames all his difficulties on his first church—especially the deacons who had promised him a nice increase in salary if the church grew, but who funded a building program instead. Pastor Bill has never owned his duplicity and his lust for material things. He is a "Resistant Christian" and is stuck on his personal journey, though he continues to preach the gospel.

Joan is a conscientious mother of two who works hard to please God. She knows her Bible as well as many pastors do. Nevertheless, she struggles with uncertainties about her salvation and knows she is stuck as a "Believing Doubter." She has given up sharing her doubts with anyone as it hurts too much when she is criticized or given pat answers.

This is a brief sampling of contemporary lives we will be examining, along with saints from the past who went through times of being stalled or stuck. We will learn from Hudson Taylor, the great missionary to China who founded the China Inland Mission. Though accomplishing much, he struggled with feelings of constant failure for *19 years* on the mission field before he discovered the "Exchanged life." Finally he learned that it was "No longer I," but rather the reality of "Christ living in [him]." His life's story was the catalyst to my epiphany experience.

How Do We Get Stalled Anyway?

Why do people get stalled on their Christian journeys? I believe there is a parallel to our physical lives. Parents are delighted with their newborn—its moving little fingers and cooing—but they also desire that the beautiful infant grow into maturity in order to experience all that life affords. But many things can obstruct the growth of the infant. Genetic, environmental, or nutritional factors can stunt physical development.

Then there is psychological maturity. Erik H. Erikson has described eight stages of psychological development. If a person does not receive the necessary care from parents in childhood, or if the person handles a particular stage in a maladaptive manner, he or she will struggle with the adverse effects for the rest of his or her life.

Growth can be scary. Many five-year-olds have clung to their mothers' skirts fearful of what they would find on their first day in school. Fear occurs at each step of growth. The high schooler can have a lot of apprehension about going to college and facing "the real world." Likewise, spiritual growth has numerous obstacles and can be scary.

Tragically, many people don't recognize there are spiritual stages of growth and, consequently, their potential loss in remaining stunted believers. Paul laments over Christians' failure to grow saying: "My dear children, for whom I am again in the pains of childbirth until Christ is formed in you…[until you]…become mature, attaining…the fullness of Christ" (Galatians 4:19; Ephesians 4:12-13 NIV). God wants us to experience maturity and the fullness of Christ living and expressing his life through us. We are afforded an amazing journey with Jesus.

As I review my spiritual journey and those of Christians around me, I see specific stages of growth. For young Christians, it is difficult to see the stages through which they will navigate in the years ahead. In fact, few even think about it. But, the more we understand our spiritual journey, the less likely we will get stuck. A roadmap will help us avoid the inevitable obstacles. Furthermore, we can learn from literature on the stages of spiritual development that goes all the way back to the third century.[6]

So far I've introduced you to a few Christians who became stalled on their spiritual pilgrimage. In the rest of this section, we will look at some of the common problems that cause individuals to get stalled or outright stuck. In the last half of the book, we will explore the seven positive stages of spiritual growth, delineating the wondrous life that enables us to overcome the obstacles and, more importantly, to experience Christ living his life through us.

Discussion Questions

1. What is your evaluation of the health of the church at large? How about your church and spiritual community?

2. Why do you think churches aren't doing a better job at producing mature followers of Christ?

3. What do you think of the notion that our spiritual growth can be stalled or stunted? Should we be concerned if we are stuck? Why?

4. What was your reaction to the specific examples the author describes? Can you think of other examples with which you are personally acquainted?

5. Have you ever been stuck in the past? If so, how did you handle it?

6. Are you stuck now? If so where?

Experiencing God's Love and Grace This Week

The epistle of Galatians describes an entire church that was stuck. Read Galatians several times this week and consider how the church got sidetracked and how the Holy Spirit, through Paul, suggests it get unstuck. If possible, read through the epistle in different translations or paraphrases. *The Message* by Eugene Peterson is especially graphic in its rendering of this book.

1

The Dutiful Christian

I was determined to have my six o'clock in the morning "quiet time," despite working 12- to 16-hour days, 7 days a week, so I put the old "Big Ben" alarm clock in a pan across the 14-foot trailer in which I was living. I'm sure it awakened everyone in the trailer park, but I'd get up, shut off the alarm, and crawl back into bed for a few more winks. I needed something more to get me up. Knowing just enough about electricity to be dangerous, I rigged up a Model-T spark coil to an alarm clock and placed two wires across the foot of my bed. The 40,000 volts launched me out of bed with a jolt, but after getting up I was only going through the motions of having a quiet time. I certainly didn't feel the presence of the Lord. I was burned out.

The story really started in high school. I was the typical teenager: interested in girls, working hard after school to buy a brand-new Chevy, neglecting my studies but enjoying life! Then I met some students who were taking their spiritual lives seriously. They challenged me to a disciplined life, so I sought out an ex-marine to disciple me. This was the beginning of my having a daily "quiet time," memorizing three Bible verses a week, and doing a weekly Bible study.

Since this was in the middle of the "Korean Conflict," I started driving to Oceanside, a town about 70 miles south of Los Angeles, to work in a Christian Businessmen's Service Center on the weekends. There I shared Christ with marines who were heading for the bloody battlefields of Korea—some never to return.

Eventually I gave up a good-paying job and moved to Oceanside to spend more time at the Servicemen's Center. I sold my pride-and-joy Chevy, bought an older car, borrowed a 14-foot trailer to live in, and supported myself by working 40 hours a week doing hard, physical labor as a hod carrier.

Every Saturday afternoon and evening, all day Sunday, and four nights during the week were spent at the Service Center. I socialized with marines on liberty by playing a variety of table games and serving them food from our free snackbar. When the opportunity presented itself, I would share Christ with them. Those who made a profession of faith were discipled. This regime gave me one free night a week—until some of the fellows asked me to start a Bible study on the base.

I had been encouraged to memorize three verses a week and decided that "if something is good, more must be better," so the three verses became six. To make sure I didn't miss something, I had a checklist that eventually included 23 items: Had I witnessed that day? Prayed? Read the Scriptures?...

But everything finally caught up with me, and I faced my Waterloo. Getting up in the morning became increasingly difficult, but when I'd go back to sleep I was plagued with guilt the rest of the day. That's when I hooked up the Model-T spark coil—but that only treated the symptoms. Exhausted, I quit my job, stopped my work at the Servicemen's Center, and moved home with my folks. I not only was burned out, but my faith had become performance-based and legalistic. It was dry, empty, and joyless—not the vibrant intimacy with Christ that he wanted for me and I desired. I had hit an "obstacle" and didn't have the foggiest idea as to what my problem was. My wheels were spinning on ice at 40 miles an hour, but I wasn't getting anywhere. I was very "active" spiritually—but stuck. Clearly, I had taken good scriptural truths and misunderstood God's intent. It would be years before I would really comprehend what had happened to me.

Getting Started on Our Spiritual Journey

When we accept Christ as our personal Savior we begin our spiritual journey, which I will be calling Stage 1. With normal growth we move on *to know* God's truths and *to do* them, which I am designating Stage 2.

Unfortunately, some Christians barely get beyond the crib— they get stalled right from the start. We will examine these "failure to thrive" infants later. However, in this, and the next several chapters, I want to address those who are at the other end of the spectrum: the many within our church walls who have a healthy appetite for God and are deeply immersed in Stage 2. They have taken to heart their walk with God and are diligently trying to know God's truths and practice them—exactly what God wants of them. But, unfortunately, something happens on their journey. Before long their Christian lives and activities start consuming them, and they sense something is wrong, but they don't know what it is.

Becoming Actively Stuck

"Actively stuck" Christians are diligently pursuing God's will, often to the point of exhaustion. They are dedicated laypeople, pastors, and missionaries who are zealous followers of Christ. They have a passion for God and his work, and they want to please him. They seem to be accomplishing much for the kingdom—God is, in fact, the most important person in their lives. But they are stuck. Their efforts to please him have led them to focus on their *activities* for God—accomplishing much for the kingdom and pleasing God by what they do. But they are busy, weary people.

They are living dutiful, if not driven lives. The dictionary definition of driven is "being under compulsion, as to succeed or excel—drivenness."[1] We want a purposeful, Christ-centered life—but not a driven life. Christ's life was purposeful, but it was not driven by compulsion. Unfortunately our best churches are filled with dutiful and driven people. Let's look at how this phenomenon develops.

Pleasing God

As serious followers of Christ, we naturally want to please God. The Scriptures clearly command this. Here are a few representative passages that speak of our pleasing him:[2]

> "Walk in a manner worthy of the Lord, to please Him in all respects, bearing fruit in every good work and increasing in the knowledge of God" (Colossians 1:10).
>
> "So we make it our goal to please him" (2 Corinthians 5:9 NIV).
>
> "Figure out what will please Christ, and then do it" (Ephesians 5:10 MSG).
>
> "Finally then, brethren, we…exhort you…to walk and please God" (1 Thessalonians 4:1).

And Christ gave us the supreme example: "And He who sent Me is with Me; He has not left Me alone, for I always do the things that are pleasing to Him" (John 8:29). In order to make progress on our spiritual journey, *it is essential that we come to the place of wanting to please God.* But then we must answer the question: *How do we please God?* We intuitively think that we please him by working hard for him and trying our best not to sin—and with that mind-set we are sure to get into trouble.

The Slippery Slope of Striving to Please God

When we try to please God by what we do, we start down a road that ends up in a very different place from where God wants us. Certainly such determination to please God seems like a noble goal. But when this is the aim, a subtle shift takes place. We start focusing on what we are *doing* to please him. Our activities and accomplishments—or lack thereof—become the center of our attention. Concentration on commendable things such as Bible study, prayer, witnessing, helping the poor, and not sinning become our objectives. Without realizing it, we have just taken a different path from the one God intended; we have started down the slippery slope—pleasing God by what we *do* for him. We are into a life of *earning God's pleasure.* The shift is subtle, but the consequences are staggering. When the primary drive and focus of our attention is on how we can please God through what we do for him, we are into earning, rule-keeping, and fleshly religion.

On top of that, the greater our desire to please, serve, and honor the Lord, the greater the potential to slip down this slope. This is especially true for those in "full-time" Christian work (that is, their financial livelihood comes through "ministry"). They have an added pressure to "perform." If you are the pastor of a church and it's not growing or you're on the mission field and can't write glowing success reports to your support base, you are more prone to question what's wrong with you and even worry that support might fall off—and, in fact, it might.

Our driven "activity" leads to relying on our efforts to achieve spiritual goals. This is the trap of all zealous religionists, and Christians aren't immune. *The universal phenomenon of religion consists of what we are accomplishing for God.* All of this can take us further down the moutain so that sometimes we lose sight of God and the people we are trying to minister too.

This reminds me of a story my wife, Betty, tells. She was in a local restaurant with our next-door neighbor Jackie. While waiting for a table, Pam, a lady in Betty's Bible study came in and the three eventually decided to have lunch together. When Pam realized that Jackie wasn't a Christian, she started presenting the "Four Spiritual Laws" to her. In fact, she became so aggressive that the atmosphere became extremely tense. When Jackie excused herself to go to the restroom, Betty explained to Pam that she and Jackie had been in dialogue on these issues for some time, and that Jackie wasn't ready to make a decision—to which Pam said, "But what if she dies in a car accident on the way home from lunch—then where will she go? And I'll be responsible!" When Jackie returned, Pam did mellow out. After she left, Jackie confided, "You know, she was more concerned that I *make a decision* than she was about me as a person." Six months later Jackie put her trust in Christ and her decision eventually touched each member of her family. Pam was driven to get Jackie to make a "decision." The activity and the result became more important than the person and being sensitive to the Holy Spirit.

The Life of the Dutiful Christian

So how do we recognize a dutiful Christian—one who is focusing on pleasing God by what he or she does for God?

Behavior becomes one's primary concern. This will naturally lead to taking one's "spiritual temperature." John Ortberg describes this phenomenon in *The Life You've Always Wanted*. He says,

> If someone asked me how my spiritual life was going, my first thought would be how I was doing at having a quiet time—praying and reading the Bible each day. If I had prayed and read the Bible for several consecutive prior days, I was likely to say that my spiritual life was going well. If not, I was likely to feel guilty and downcast. So prayer and Bible study became the gauge of my spiritual condition.[3]

He concludes that this measures one's spiritual life in "superficial ways."

Avoiding Sin

The dutiful Christian will work hard not to sin. Our desire to please God by not sinning is a worthy endeavor. And I am certainly not advocating sin. But the focus is wrong. Such an emphasis may help us deal with sin, but in the process it often leads to pride and hypocrisy or guilt and failure.

Furthermore, if we are somewhat successful in eradicating sin from our lives, at least certain sins that we are monitoring, it is easy to overlook others that aren't on our radar screen. We might eliminate adultery, drunkenness, theft, and lying, and never notice pride, control, greed, or judgmentalism.

Keeping the Rules

As we focus on the things we should and should not do for God, we are into "rule-keeping," aka legalism. It makes no difference how altruistic and noble the activities are for God and how despicable the things we are avoiding are. The focus and motive define the behavior. Legalism seeks to earn God's favor by what we do for him. Pastor Steve McVey elaborates:

> Any approach to Christian living that focuses on keeping rules as a means of experiencing victory or growing spiritually is legalism. Legalism is a system in which a person seeks to gain God's acceptance or blessings by what [one] does....Is your concept of the Christian life one which suggests that God's primary concern with you is your behavior? If so, you are a card-carrying member of the Legalist Lodge. God's concern with you isn't about rules but relationship. When you properly understand your relationship to God, the rules tend to take care of themselves. But when your focus is on the rules, spiritual failure is certain.[4]

When our mode of operation no longer flows from a trust and love relationship but rather functions out of duty, we are into "religion"—a religion of legalism and not relationship. Legalism is a harsh taskmaster. It's like addiction. At first it can be very gratifying, but it always demands more and eventually leads to defeat. Paul says, "Rule-keeping does not naturally evolve into living by faith, but only perpetuates itself in more and more rule-keeping, a fact observed in Scripture" (Galatians 3:12 MSG). A legalist person's life will be driven by oughts, shoulds, and musts. An endless "to do" list will hang over his head. The authors of *True-Faced* comment on this phenomenon, saying "We arrive at *The Room of Good Intentions* out of a determination or inner drive to please God. But in that room, we discover we never can do enough to please him."[5]

Rule-keeping will shrivel up our love relationship with God to the delight of Satan. When that happens, our hearts become dry and worship becomes perfunctory. Our love affair with God is reduced to a series of chores.

Markers of Spiritual Success

Taking one's spiritual temperature and keeping the rules become measurable markers of spiritual success. I certainly fell prey to this for a number of decades. Let me illustrate how this developed with my Scripture memorization. Hiding God's Word in our hearts is a command of God and an important tool in maturing in Christ. Goals have a place in our lives. But human nature, being what it is, can quickly turn the loftiest spiritual goals into a rule or "the law." Before long, instead of those verses helping me look to Christ, I began looking at how many verses I had memorized the previous week. If I succeeded in reaching my goal, I felt good about what I had done. When I failed, I felt guilty. After awhile the focal point was more about how well I was succeeding in my weekly goal of memorizing verses. Though I didn't realize it at the time, a quantum shift had taken place. I had moved from a trust and love relationship with Christ to a work-oriented means to "please God." Whenever we shift *our focus to our accomplishments to please him, we move to a performance-based religion.*

Though I never conceptualized it in such terms, I believe the activity of memorizing Scripture became a marker of spiritual success. How did this happen? I started out with the correct heart motive—to do what God wanted me to do. But heart motives and attitudes are not quantifiable, whereas works in the Christian life lend themselves to evaluation and measurement—and herein lays a problem. We have an understandable tendency to focus on what we can quantify and measure, and our heart attitude gets lost in the process. Furthermore, we like to have concrete results that can easily lead to our comparing ourselves with *our* predetermined standards or those encouraged by others. To add to the pressure, our Western culture thrives on quantifying and evaluating progress and success. *Since God hasn't given us a marker of spiritual success, we create our own.*

So the new Christian, out of a healthy response to please God, starts to focus on the external. In one way or another, we are indoctrinated with all that we need *to know* and *to do* as an obedient Christian. When these tasks are added to a schedule already heavy with getting an education, earning a living, or raising a family, life becomes burdensome. Instead of Jesus' yoke being "easy" and his load "light," the burden of the Christian life becomes crushing, and we grow exhausted. Christ came to deliver us from such a life!

A Romans 7 Existence

When I was stuck in Stage 2—knowing God's truths and doing them—there were many successes, and I often felt good about my walk with the Lord. But I also experienced a lot of guilt and failure. For example, during those years I always did a written, weekly Bible study that included a personal application (how does this passage apply to me or how am I going to incorporate what I learned this week into my life?). "I need to be more faithful" and "I should do more for the Lord" repeated themselves like the refrains of a song. "I will spend more time reviewing verses." "I will spend more time in prayer." "I will witness more adamantly." There were hundreds of these applications, and almost all of them centered around knowing God's Word better or being more diligent in doing it: *to know* and *to do.* Far too often duty characterized my walk with God and, not infrequently, it turned into drudgery. Oh, there were times of victory, but more often than not I felt I wasn't measuring up.

When we are living our Christian life on the basis of rules, we incarcerate ourselves into a "Romans 7 existence." Much of the time I felt, "I am not practicing what I would like to do.…Evil is present in me....Wretched man that I am! Who will set me free?" (Romans 7:15,21,24). (Readers who believe Romans 7 doesn't apply to the Christian may substitute Galatians 5:16-25, which clearly applies to the Christian and has a parallel message.) I was living on the basis of what I "ought" to do rather than on the basis of a loving response to God's love. Too often the very obligation to *do* things for God kept me *from* God. My heart became dry and the Christian life a grind. I would dedicate myself again and again— only to fail. It would be a stretch to say I experienced the "abundant life." Now, as I look back on my journey, I can see that God had so much more for me, but I was oblivious to it at the time.

The Elder Brother

I have really been describing the prodigal son's elder brother, who was a hard-working, loyal son. He thought he was working hard for his father, when in actuality he was working for himself. He tried to earn what was already his, but which he *never* was able to receive. He failed because he chose the road to *earning his father's pleasure* rather than what I will later refer to as *"faithing"* his father's pleasure, to *earn his father's love* rather than *receiving and giving love.* One road leads to a party in God's presence; the other to exhaustion from hard work, bitterness of heart, and totally missing God's love and joy. The elder brother, outside the house complaining, stands as a classic example of one who is stuck as a dutiful servant. He never became who he was. Unfortunately there are a lot of wonderful, hard-working Christians like the elder brother who are missing the party.[6]

God Has Something Better for Us

There must be something better—and there is! Dallas Willard says,

The genius of the moral teachings of Jesus and his first students was his insistence that you cannot keep the law by trying not to break the law. That will only make a Pharisee of you and sink you into layers of hypocrisy. Instead, you have to be transformed in the functions of the soul so that the deeds of the law are a natural outflow of who you have become.[7]

God does not want us to live a Romans 7 existence, to live out of the abilities of our own lives. He has given us a new heart and life and wants us to experience a gracious life without condemnation, a "Romans 8 life"—an abundant life.

Christ's invitation is clear:

Are you tired? Worn out? Burned out on religion? Come to me. Get away with me and you'll recover your life. I'll show you how to take a real rest. Walk with me and work with me—watch how I do it. Learn the unforced rhythms of grace. I won't lay anything heavy or ill-fitting on you. Keep company with me and you'll learn to live freely and lightly (Matthew 11:28-30 MSG).

You May Be Stuck in a Performance-Based Christianity If...

1. You are trying to please God by what you do.

2. Your focus is more on what you have or have not done for God, than God himself.

3. Your Christian life seems to be a constant struggle.

4. You are very active in your Christian life—but something seems to be missing.

Discussion Questions

1. The author makes the radical statement that our best churches are filled with dutiful and driven people. What do you think of this notion?

2. How can you tell if your working hard for God is an activity of the flesh?

3. Do you agree with the statement that the greater our desire to please, serve, and honor the Lord, the greater the potential to slip down the slope of trying to earn God's pleasure?

4. If you set aside a time for a daily quiet time, are you into rule-keeping and legalism?

5. Do you think striving to please God by what you do is really the wrong emphasis? What can make it right, and what makes it wrong?

6. The author says the elder brother "never became who he was." What does that statement mean?

Experiencing God's Love and Grace This Week

Find a quiet place and for 15 to 30 minutes read the story of the prodigal son several times slowly (Luke 15:11-32). Ask God to enlighten you through the Holy Spirit. Imagine yourself in the scene. Think about each person in the story and what the emotions and feelings might be at each point in the account. First consider the father, then the prodigal, and finally the older brother. Reflect on others not mentioned but who certainly are part of the story, such as the mother and the townspeople. Finally, consider with whom you identify and what might God be telling you.

In addition you might want to get a copy of *TrueFaced* and read chapter 5. It elaborates on the contrast between pleasing God and trusting him. It is well worth your attention.[8]

2

The Corporate Christian

The most productive church or Christian organization, from a human perspective, is run like a large corporation. This is not inherently good or bad—it just is. But just as God warned Samuel, so the church needs to be aware that there are significant risks to both the leaders and followers when power is accumulated and centralized (1 Samuel 8:5-22).

Before we look at the risks, I want to make it clear that the "corporate church" or any "corporate body of believers" has many significant benefits. God ordained Christian fellowship because we need each other. Churches, as well as many parachurch organizations, have been given by God to facilitate our growth. Far too many Christians live purposeless lives, but Christian organizations can motivate and give meaning by providing direction, affirmation, security, and camaraderie—all essential for the believer's growth. In addition, a group of believers can organize, pool resources, and accomplish more for the kingdom of God than individuals functioning alone. And many organizations are doing an exemplary job in furthering God's work. These are some of the benefits, now let's look at some of the hazards.

The Corporate Body Can Slide Down the Slippery Slope

God typically uses key individuals or groups to guide us in a vital relationship with him. This may be a pastor, friend, church, or a Christian organization. Such an individual or group becomes our spiritual leader or family and is an important part of our growth process. When we are blessed by a mentor, we soak up what he or she teaches. Paul encouraged such mentoring with his instruction to "be ye followers of me even as I also am of Christ" (1 Corinthians 11:1 KJV).

Mentors as Models

The single most important mentor in my life was a Christian organization called "The Navigators," which encouraged the basics in Christian growth and discipleship—so I aspired to be a model "Navigator." I fervently followed in their footsteps, studying hard and sharing what I learned. But now as I look back, it is interesting to note some of the incidentals that I also picked up along the way. Fifty years ago most of the leaders had a specific style of black Bible with wide margins for personal notes, but without "study helps"…as they might adversely influence a reader's thinking. There also was a unique "ladder" drawn on the edge of the Bible to facilitate the quick location of a passage. We carried a certain sized black notebook for our Bible studies and the characteristic "Memory Pack" to hold the verses we were learning. It became important to have all these items—they became status symbols of a "good" Navigator. You may smile at this (and I do too) but most individuals well immersed in Stage 2 of growth—knowing God's truths and doing them—probably have comparable modeling, though it may look different from the one I am describing.

I will ever be grateful to Dawson Trotman and the Navigators for the many positive influences on my life. But immersing oneself deeply into any group has potential liabilities. As you have already seen in the previous chapter, I applied "good things" to the point that they became counterproductive in my life. All of the commendable disciplines that I learned from the Navigators fed my tendency to work hard by the flesh to please God and man. Unfortunately, both the leader and follower are seldom aware of the powerful influence being exerted.

Conformity Required

When one is immersed in Stage 2, what the mentors teach is "gospel," and conformity becomes crucial. Mentors and their zealous followers thrive in this environment. In fact, in any cohesive group, there tends to be a "group think," that is, pressure—albeit subtle—to think and act a certain way.[1] Answers tend to be pretty clear-cut. Generally a person is taught not to question—at least outside certain boundaries—but to learn the "right answers." What someone should think and do is very clear.

In fact, most Christian groups have a long list of acceptable and unacceptable beliefs and behaviors. To be affirmed you must follow the guidelines. If the truth were known, everyone transgresses some of the time; however, if you acknowledge failure, you aren't accepted. So pleasing people becomes all-important, which propels us to focus on our *activity* for God—to be seen and approved by others. This system lends itself to recognition, accolades, and ego gratification. If one works hard and doesn't ask the hard questions, acceptance is generally assured and yields a lot of mutual admiration—and that feels very good. But woe to the person who thinks outside the box.

"Christian Corporations" Are Here to Produce

The "corporate body," whether it is a church or parachurch organization, is bound together to *accomplish certain things* for God. This is good. But once this has consciously or unconsciously become the *goal*, our motive often subtly shifts from focusing on God to focusing on what we are *doing* for God. Our Western culture thrives on success by quantifying results. This exerts a lot of pressure for Christian leaders and followers to produce an impressive "bottom line."

Measurable Markers of Corporate Success

Just as the "Dutiful Christian" can take his or her spiritual temperature and have measurable markers of spiritual success, a group of individuals united together as a church or parachurch organization will invariably evaluate how it is doing. Such "measurable markers" may be attendance, first-time decisions for Christ, number of people being discipled, number of baptisms, missionary budget, programs offered, seating capacity of the sanctuary, or the size of the budget.

I remember sitting with a group of Christian leaders and being given a sheet of paper to list the goals of the Christian organization, and then to list the "measurable markers" that would verify the accomplishment of those goals. This is not necessarily wrong—but it is problematic. It encourages us to focus on the external, which excludes the heart. And before long our egos are attached to all the fine things we are doing for God, and that can further erode our heart relationship with God.

To *focus* on these measurable results leads the "corporate church" or "the corporate body of believers" to operate more like a business than the family of God. We end up promoting a product instead of a Person. We are now—at best—working to earn God's pleasure, and—at worst—working to gain applause and pleasure for ourselves. This can become addicting, which adds to the tendency to get stuck here. The individual becomes what I am calling a "Corporate Christian" if he or she is involved in this process.

On one hand, everything the corporate body of believers is doing can be good; on the other hand, it can all be wood, hay, and stubble—in fact, idolatry. *All of these works can be scriptural, and all can be of the flesh.*

The Consequences of Sliding Down the Slope

The Program Can Become More Important Than the Person

When the corporate system is functioning well and producing the desired results, individuals can get lost in the process. It is almost like the religious conflict of Christ's day regarding the Sabbath. God made the Sabbath for man, the Pharisees made man for the Sabbath (see Mark 2:27). In some instances the "corporation," whether it is a church or parachurch organization, can become more important than the parishioner. As Michael J. Wilkins describes in the book *In His Image:*

> It is a tragedy, then, when our institutions become more important than the individual—when the individual is made to serve the institution. Then supporting the institution becomes the end, and the individual is the means to the end....Because my end goal was numbers, not always depth, I considered our church activities more important than the spiritual growth of the people who made up the church....Are we making people into disciples *of our institutions,* or are our institutions making people into *disciples of Jesus?* Are our disciples proficient at running *programs* or at living a real *relationship* with Jesus?[2]

Performance

Our efforts for God can easily be turned into a performance to be seen by others. We are warned: "Be especially careful when you are trying to be good so that you don't make a performance out of it" (Matthew 6:1 MSG). We would never call it performance, but that can easily become the essence of what we are doing. The authors of *The Critical Journey*, when referring to this stage of growth, say, "Life becomes a performance, an act, a play, a drama in which we are the leading persons....We cannot be vulnerable or look weak in front of others because we would be out of control....We thrive on the audience reaction. Their applause becomes addictive....We are ultimately very, very lonely people."[3]

Michael Wilkins, a pastor and seminary dean, goes on to make this profound statement: "I believe that the number one problem of pastors and pastoral staff in the local church is that they don't love their people. Instead, they fall prey to the disease of performance. They lead by performing well."[4] I don't believe we need to single out pastors; we are all capable of falling prey to the disease of performance. And, unfortunately, it's contagious.

Building Monuments to Ourselves

When we focus on *serving* God we remain in control. Our kingdom can remain intact; our ego remains on the throne. We can continue our incessant pursuit to build a monument to ourselves, and we can do it all in the name of Christ! We study the Scriptures, build a ministry, devise a plan, and carry it out, all the time remaining in charge. David Benner addresses this by saying:

> [The] problem in simply trying to do what God asks is that it leaves the kingdom of self intact. I remain in control, and my willful ways of running my life remain unchallenged. The whole point of the kingdom of God is to overturn the kingdom of self. These are two rival spiritual kingdoms. We need to be very suspicious when...control and egocentricity are left unchallenged in our Christ-following.[5]

Competing with God

When we build monuments to ourselves or our organization, we start competing with God. It seems revolting to even suggest that we might consider competing with God—we would never think about it in those terms. But I wonder if sometimes that is how God sees it. Eugene Peterson says, "For life's basic decision is rarely, if ever, whether to believe in God or not, but whether to worship or compete with him."[6] Competing with God sounds pretty crass, nevertheless God verbalized this very concern saying: "lest Israel claim glory for itself against Me" (Judges 7:2 NKJV). This is easily what we can slip into when we start focusing on what "we have done for him" and what our Christian comrades see and think about us.

An Environment of Guilt

In an environment that focuses on results, the primary instrument used to motivate people is guilt, which in the short haul is a lot easier to use and may seem to produce more results than modeling or inspiration. But guilt—especially guilt induced by people—does not motivate the heart. Therein lies another giant problem. When we motivate by guilt, we have assumed for ourselves the role of the Holy Spirit. This in turn produces works of the flesh in ourselves and in the people we are trying to influence. The authors of *The Sacred Romance* say, "So many of our contemporary churches operate on this same system of guilt. When our people are crying out for communion and rest, we ask them to teach another Sunday-school class. When they falter under the load, we admonish them with Scriptures on serving others."[7] Typically this approach results in the callous folks shrugging it off and the weary working harder.

Busyness

Busyness is the inevitable result of the environment we have been discussing. The Chinese word for busyness is made up of two characters that represent: "to kill" and "heart." Busyness will kill the heart, but sometimes it works the other way around—if something is lacking in our heart relationship with God, we bury the problem by busyness. This only aggravates our predicament. Any heartfelt sensitivity and responsiveness to God becomes so dulled by our busyness that we become oblivious to his still, small voice. In the words of Henri Nouwen, "Our task is to help people concentrate on the real but often hidden event of God's active presence in their lives. Hence the question that must guide all organizing activity in a parish is not how to keep people busy, but how to keep them from being so busy that they can no longer hear the voice of God who speaks in silence."[8]

One of Satan's major techniques against conscientious, dedicated Christians is to keep them so busy they are exhausted and unable to hear God's voice. John Eldredge comments on the power of busyness to overcome us:

> Hyenas cannot bring down a lion in its prime. What they do is run it and taunt it and wear it down to the point of exhaustion. Once they see it cannot defend itself, then they close in. The strategy of our Enemy in the age we live in now is *busyness* and *drivenness*. Ask the people you know how things are going. Nine out of ten will answer something to the effect of "really busy." ...The deadly scheme is this: *keep them running. That way, they'll never take care of their hearts. We'll burn them out and take them out.*[9]

Pastor Steve McVey describes his experience: "I found myself becoming more and more consumed with ministry and less and less with Jesus....The work of the ministry gradually became my life."[10] This is exactly the trap in which Israel found itself. Paul comments:

> And Israel, who seemed so interested in reading and talking about what God was doing, missed it. How could they miss it? Because instead of trusting God, *they* took over. They were absorbed in what they themselves were doing. They were so absorbed in their "God projects" that they didn't notice God right in front of them (Romans 9:31-32 MSG).

Hiding

When we focus on how hard we are working for God, it may, for a time lead to pride. However, it more commonly leads to a conscious or unconscious sense of failure, which propels us to hide and wear a mask. Leaders have more to lose and, therefore, are more prone to hide. We will hide our true selves from others and sometimes even ourselves. In fact, if we are living in a performance-based environment, such hiding is fostered because any truly honest soul will be soundly judged and found wanting. We need to learn the importance of transparency, of coming to God with all our weaknesses and being honest and open with a few trustworthy Christians. The choice between hiding or disclosing a sin, weakness, question, or even a negative feeling, often provides a good indicator as to whether one is stuck in Stage 2. This is true for the leader and the follower. People focused on doing will typically be hiding their inadequacies or questions—but of course they will hide that fact if they are aware of it. Unfortunately, they may not even be aware of their hiding since it has become such a normal mode of operation.

To Sum Up

Roy and Revel Hession, in *We Would See Jesus,* depict this so well:

> To concentrate on service and activity for God may often actively thwart our attaining of the true goal, God Himself....Christian service of itself can and so often does, leave our self-centered nature untouched....In this condition we are trying to give to others an answer which we have not truly and deeply found for ourselves. The tragedy is that much of the vast network of Christian activity and service is bent on propagating an answer for people's needs and problems which few of those propagating it are finding adequate in their own lives. We need to leave our lusting for ever-larger spheres of Christian service and concentrate on seeing God for ourselves and finding the deep answer for life in Him. Then, even if we are located in the most obscure corner of the globe, the world will make a road to our door to get that answer. Our service of help to our fellows then becomes incidental to our vision of God....This does not mean that God does not want us engaged actively in His service. He does; but His purpose is often far different from what we think.[11]

You May Be Stuck at Stage 2 of Your Journey If...

1. You are prone to hide a sin, weakness, questions, or even negative feelings from others, especially close Christian friends.

2. Your focus is more on programs, performance, and achievements than on Christ.

3. You are more concerned with what other Christians think of you than what Christ thinks of you.

4. You're exhausted from your Christian activities.

Discussion Questions

1. To what extent are you in an environment that is guilt inducing? What are some examples of guilt-inducing statements that might trouble the more sensitive among us?

2. What are your personal markers of spiritual or religious success? What are the markers in your religious community?

3. Is there a place for "measurable markers"? Elaborate.

4. If a "successful corporate church" discarded its focus on measurable spiritual markers and modeled a life focused on Christ, would it gain or lose members? Explain.

5. Has an individual or group been important in your personal growth? To what extent have you identified with that person or group? What has been helpful and unhelpful in the relationship?

6. Does the group you are in foster conformity of thought and actions? How do they do that? To what extent is that good or harmful?

Experiencing God's Love and Grace This Week

I encourage you to read Ephesians chapters 1–3 daily and dwell on God's phenomenal love. Focus on God and his love for you. Reading from different translations may further help you appreciate his grace. One time read it through slowly out loud and in place of every pronoun put your own name. Pray the two prayers (1:17-19 and 3:16-21) for yourself.

3

The Expert Christian

The greatest temptation for the dedicated Christian is not power, prestige, accomplishments, wealth, or even sex. The most seductive enticement is knowledge and the need to be right—*religiously right*. It was the tree of the knowledge of good and evil so they would be like gods that first got Adam and Eve into trouble, and it is an allurement to which all religionists since then have fallen prey.

In the previous two chapters we have seen how a focus on pleasing God can result in working hard to earn God's pleasure through fleshly means. Now we'll look at how the same dynamic added to the human need to be the cauldron of truth can result in our getting stuck in a slightly difference place—becoming an "Expert Christian."

The subtle shift typically starts when we unconsciously shift our focus from *knowing the God of all truth* to *knowing the truth about God*. Our major concern has shifted from the *Living Word* to the *written Word*. Instead of focusing our attention on being *Christlike*, it is now on being *doctrinally right*. The difference might seem minuscule, but the effects are monumental. The moment that knowing truth becomes more important than knowing the God of all truth we are in trouble. We have shifted our focal point and allegiance and have embarked down a different road.

You quickly protest, "Isn't doctrine important?" My response: "It's not only important; it's crucial." Others object, "If one properly applies doctrine, won't that solve all of these problems?" My response: "Yes, and doctrine that is properly applied will exalt Christ above everything else." But, unfortunately, too often we focus on doctrine and obscure the aim of all sound doctrine—Christ.

Doctrine Is Crucial

Some individuals totally deemphasize doctrine. They have been called the no-creed creedalists. They protest against an emphasis on creed over Christ, but that in itself is a creed. The fact is that we all hold to some doctrine, whether we are aware of it or not. I first struggled with this in medical school, so I wrote down what I believed to be the basic, essential doctrines on which I could not compromise. I ended up with a list of five short statements. These were nonnegotiable. Anyone who knows me well knows that I will fight and die for these essential truths. There is a time and place to contend for the truth of the faith—to be a *defender of God's truth*. Jude emphasizes the importance of sound doctrine, writing to "Christians everywhere" and "urging [them] to stoutly defend the truth that God gave once for all to his people to keep without change through the years" (Jude 1:3 TLB). Doctrine is crucial, and at times it is incumbent on us to defend the truth.

Then What's the Problem?

Doctrine is like salt in our bodies. The normal amount of sodium in the body must remain between the narrow range of 136 and 145 (mEq/L). This is essential for health and life. If the sodium varies only a few percentage points outside this range, it not only causes illness, but quickly can cause death. And it doesn't matter if the level is too high or too low; either is equally damaging. Likewise, spiritually, a certain amount of the right doctrine is essential for spiritual health. But get too little or too much or hold on to it in the wrong way, and it will squeeze spiritual vitality right out of you and those you influence.

Focus

Doctrine can get out of balance in countless ways. One such way is to focus excessively on it. It's similar to the way some patients focus excessively on their bodies, thus aggravating their physical problems and often creating new ones. Our bodies function best when we treat them properly without fixating on them. Spiritually we need to embrace doctrines that are clearly and repeatedly enumerated in the Scriptures, but it's essential to keep our focus upon Christ.

An obsession with correct doctrine puts the focus in the wrong place. As British theologian Alister McGrath warns, "The Bible is not primarily a doctrinal sourcebook."[1] Christ said to the religious leaders of the day, "You have your heads in your Bibles constantly because you think you'll find eternal life there. But you miss the forest for the trees. These Scriptures are all about *me!* And here I am, standing right before you, and you aren't willing to receive from me the life you say you want" (John 5:39-40 MSG). Our primary focus needs to be on *the Living Word*—Christ.

Elaborating on the Scriptures

In the time of Christ, the religious leaders rightfully placed great importance on the *Torah*—the five books of law in the Old Testament. In their zeal to fully comply with their scriptures, they developed and then put in writing the 800-page *Mishnah* that elaborated on the *Torah*. For instance, it spells out 39 specific things necessary to keep the Sabbath holy. And if that wasn't enough, they developed and wrote the *Talmud*, which added to the *Mishnah* and became 18 volumes long. We wouldn't think about doing that today—or would we?

In the religious environment I grew up in, dancing, lipstick, reading the comics on Sunday, alcohol, and all motion pictures were considered sin. I remember hearing detailed "biblical" explanations as to why each of these was contrary to God's written Word. These "sins" are now pretty well debunked in many Christian communities. But even now we don't have to go very far to find numerous rules, laws, and injunctions in the Christian community. There are certain doctrinal statements we had better not question. Halloween is clearly of the devil. In many circles the so-called five points of Calvinism are as authoritative, and sometimes more authoritative, than the Bible itself—though no one would ever admit that.[2] And if you aren't a Republican could you even be a Christian? (Of course, there are other branches of the church that assume all true Christians are Democrats and/or pacifists!) Now, I am not an advocate of Halloween, I believe most of what Calvin taught, and I am a registered Republican who usually votes the party line. But if you or I don't give the right answer on these and sundry other issues, we'll receive harsh judgment—by God's people.

In recent decades, evangelicalism has put *living a separated life* in a backseat to its emphasis on what one believes. In fact, it's my opinion, that the *"Believe-Right Gospel"* is the most important concern for the "Expert Christian." Many of our Christian communities show little tolerance for any divergence in what a person may believe.

Closely related to this elevation of a created set of teachings is a tendency to elevate the Bible to such an extent that it effectively overshadows Christ. Somehow we need to figure out how to hold true to the Scriptures while we exalt Christ and maintain an ear attentive to the Holy Spirit.

Systems of Theology

Interrelated with all of this is the desire to understand God and doctrine—to master it and put it into a definable, comprehensive package. This is a noble and appropriate desire, but we must recognize and accept its limitations. For "now we see things imperfectly as in a poor mirror, but then we will see everything with perfect clarity. All that I know now is partial and incomplete, but then I will know everything completely" (1 Corinthians 13:12 NLT). I believe that either God didn't want us to have all the answers or else our minds are incapable of fully grasping it all (Isaiah 55:8-9). It may well be that our spiritual capacity is as limited as a two-dimensional understanding of a three-dimensional world. The Scriptures speak about mystery. God's ways are higher than our ways. He won't allow us to put him or his truths in a box—there will always be something that won't quite fit. God will not allow us to fully understand him or to comprehensively systematize him. God's strongest rebuke of Job was over this very issue (Job 42:1-6).

Any *systematized* form of theology tends to emphasize certain passages that rightly promote that theology's position on a doctrine, but it often minimizes, ignores, or explains away another body of Scripture that seems to say something different. Systematic theologies do this whether they advocate Calvinism, Arminianism, Open Theology, or whatever. I believe we all have a right to hold positions on the many topics of theology. But we must hold such *systems* of thought somewhat loosely. Lest I be misunderstood, let me be very clear on this point. We are to hold to the Scriptures firmly. It is the human conclusions—interpretations, explanations, and summarizations of the Scriptures—that I am advocating we hold loosely. *They must never be on par with the Scriptures and certainly never supersede the Scriptures.*

Every truth in the Scriptures must be held in the *context* of the entire Word of God (Acts 20:27 KJV). G. Campbell Morgan said, "The whole truth does not lie in 'It is written,' but in 'It is written' and 'Again it is written.' The second text must be placed over against the first to balance it and give it symmetry, just as the right wing must work along with the left to balance the bird and enable it to fly."[3]

I am not against systematized theology. It can help us organize and get a grasp on the entire Word of God. It also gives us a certain sense of security. But if such a system becomes a grid through which we look at Scripture and interpret the Scripture, *it will limit the ability of the Holy Spirit to teach us.* Therefore any systematic approach must be held loosely in at least three ways: First, we must recognize that opposing viewpoints often contain some truth to be considered. Thus, we need to remain open to evaluate individual doctrines in light of all of Scripture, accepting that no one system can encompass the whole of truth of God. If we cannot dialogue with others from different traditions that still claim Jesus as their Savior, we are probably holding our systems of theology more tightly than Christ. Second, something has gone awry in our theology if protecting or enforcing our system of beliefs comes at the expense of people and relationships. Doctrine shouldn't take priority over love.

Third, and most critically—and perhaps attention to this will keep it all in proper perspective—we must be careful that our doctrinal systems do not interfere with our love relationship with God. Our theology should *enhance* our romance with God. If it doesn't, we need to be suspicious. If it is primarily cognitive, God will get left out.

Theologian A.W. Tozer elaborates on some of the reasons for this phenomenon: "The text became the test of orthodoxy, and Fundamentalism, the most influential school of evangelical Christianity, went over to textualism. The inner life was neglected in a constant preoccupation with the 'truth,' and truth was interpreted to mean doctrinal truth only. No other meaning of the word was allowed. Objectivism had won. The human heart cowered in its cold cellar, ashamed to show its face."[4] This is a sad commentary on which I believe Christ would have a lot to say were he walking the earth today.

Results of Being a Connoisseur of God's Truth

What are the results of zealous Christians focusing on doctrine rather than Christ? William Barclay says, "It is when people are really in earnest and their beliefs really matter to them, that they are apt to get up against each other. The greater their enthusiasm, the greater the danger that they may collide."[5] Unfortunately, we in the Christian community are too often known for our contentiousness rather than our love—both among ourselves and to the world at large. An unforeseen legacy of our "Reformation focus on Scripture alone" has been a heritage of ever-splintering groups that each claim to further identify the real truth of Scripture. The result is 33,800 different Christian denominations, each claiming to be "right."[6]

The collisions of differing theologies cause damage in several ways.

Judgmentalism

The expert on God's truth must be exceedingly careful lest he or she gets mired in judgmentalism. At least two factors tend to grease the judgmental skids for the individual stuck as an "Expert Christian." First, if he or she is stuck here the individual has not matured in his or her personal interactive relationship with Christ. This deficiency in the life of faith and adoration often manifests itself when doctrine is elevated over love. Furthermore, having progressed this far, he or she has an excellent knowledge of the Scriptures, and such knowledge can have a tendency to lead to arrogance (see 1 Corinthians 8:1). Lest we forget our history, there were centuries when professing Christians fought against and killed those who held doctrinally differing views— those who didn't "believe right." Even the great reformer John Calvin had some complicity in the death of an individual who held a differing doctrinal view.[7] Klaus Issler comments:

> German theologian Helmut Thielicke notes how theological knowledge can be used for the purposes of self-exaltation. "Anyone who deals with truth…succumbs all too easily to the psychology of the possessor….In his reflective detachment the theologian feels himself superior….[This] is a real *spiritual disease.*"…For any position of leadership and responsibility, the greatest temptations are pride and self-exaltation.[8]

An additional issue is always the speck and the log: "Do not judge so that you will not be judged. For in the way you judge, you will be judged….Why do you look at the speck that is in your brother's eye, but do not notice the log that is in your own eye?" (Matthew 7:1-4). From a psychological point of view, our very strong reactions often result from our own personal insecurity or an insecurity about the position we are defending.

What we criticize in others often has a relationship to what is deeply buried within us.

Mean Christians

If we are *experts of God's truth*, it might seem appropriate that we would have righteous indignation about the issues and the offenders of God's truth. But if we are stuck at Stage 2, we are much more likely to just be *mean*, whether mean toward the world at large or to a Christian brother or sister. Dallas Willard addresses individuals who get into conflicts over issues within the church, saying that it leads to "righteously mean Christians. In fact, standing on these things as essential is what produces mean and angry Christians. This is an inevitable result of failing to center everything on becoming people who have the character of Christ." He goes on to quote a Christian college president as saying, "'It is difficult to be a Christian in a secular world....But, you know, it is sometimes more difficult to be a leader in Christian circles.'...Christians are routinely taught by example and word that it is more important to be right...than it is to be Christ-like. In fact, being right licenses you to be mean, and indeed, requires you to be mean—righteously mean, of course."[9]

Dried-Up Hearts

Unfortunately, "Expert Christianity" dries up our hearts and steals our joy, which adds to the vicious cycle we are in. Centering our lives on the truth of God rather than the God of truth makes the Word a dry set of data rather than a love letter. It may boost our egos to master its contents, but it will not thrill our souls or increase our love and joy. A.W. Tozer comments,

> Sound Bible exposition is an imperative *must* in the Church of the Living God....But exposition may be carried on in such

a way as to leave the hearers devoid of any true spiritual nourishment whatever. For it is not mere words that nourish the
soul, but God Himself, and unless and until the hearers find
God in personal experience they are not the better for having
heard the truth. The Bible is not an end in itself, but a means to
bring [people] to an intimate and satisfying knowledge of God,
that they may enter into Him, that they may delight in His Presence, may taste and know the inner sweetness of the very
God Himself in the core and center of their hearts.[10]

Avoiding the "Expert Christian" Trap

So what is the solution? How can one avoid being or becoming
an "Expert Christian"? It starts with a willingness to give up the
self-gratifying role of being an expert of God's truth and to accept
the fact that we are all pilgrims on this spiritual journey. We need
to "clothe [ourselves] with humility" (1 Peter 5:5). It certainly
involves honesty with ourselves and others about what is going on
in our own lives and the realization that none of us even comes
close to having absolute knowledge about God's truth.

Furthermore, I believe many of us who are stuck at this point
in our pursuit of God are totally oblivious to the fact that we are
in a rut or that we need to progress any further in our spiritual
journey. Thus, we all need to ask God to search our hearts in this
matter (Psalm 139:23-24). Then we need to take deliberate steps
to grow in our spiritual comprehension and willingness to act on
what we believe. In addition, there are some specific issues that I
would suggest the person prone to being an "Expert Christian"
may want to consider.

Knowing and Owning What You Don't Know

In medicine it is sometimes said that the biggest problem is
not knowing what you don't know. My daughter had leukemia,

and after a bone marrow transplant she suffered from months of painful rashes. Her oncologist was an expert in transplants but not in treating rashes. It took our insisting that our daughter obtain the opinion of a dermatologist to remedy the situation. The oncologist didn't know how much he didn't know. We need to be humble enough to admit that there is a lot that all of us don't understand about God and his precepts. And that's okay; it is no sin. None of us has a clear understanding of all truth. The sin is when we think we know what we don't know.

In "Make Room for Mystery," a chapter in *The Root of Righteousness*, Tozer says:

> The beginner in Christ will not have read long in the Scriptures till he comes upon passages that appear to contradict each other....He may do one of several things....He may consult some...theologians who in fancied near-omniscience presume to resolve all Biblical difficulties....This...is sure to be fatal to true spirituality....Far better...is the humility that admits its ignorance and waits quietly on God for His own light to appear in His own time....No one should be ashamed to admit that he does not know, and no Christian should fear the effect of such a confession.[11]

Change Your Approach to the Scriptures

There are many different ways to approach the Scriptures. We can study the Bible for knowledge, guidance, encouragement, and nourishment. We can be motivated out of simple curiosity, questions, fear, duty, and love. We can utilize our head or our heart or both. We can approach God's Word with openness or biases—a desire to know what God would tell us or a need to confirm what we already believe and want to prove is true.

Some people have studied the Bible a great deal, yet far too often they have missed the author. Klaus Issler quotes a seminary professor who, during a crisis, found the Bible inadequate to his need. Issler comments on this man's dilemma:

> The problem is not with the Bible—it is God's revelation to us, the vibrant and living Word of God, inspired by the Spirit of God. The problem stems from approaching the Bible only at a cognitive or historical level. Scripture must be studied within the context of a dynamic and growing relationship with the God who is personal and who is intimately and supernaturally involved in the everyday aspects of his children....Such divine guidance requires many of us to color outside the line from our customary view of God, to permit him to impact our experience as he so chooses.[12]

Many stuck in this second stage of growth focus on certain portions of the Scriptures such as Paul's epistles, prophecy, or Old Testament law. These people may need to rediscover Christ in the Gospels and the book of Psalms. What is crucial is that the Scriptures be approached with an open heart and a desire to have a dynamic, living relationship with the author of the Bible. We need to delight in his presence and taste and see that he is good (Psalm 34:8). Anything less will leave us wanting.

Lifting Up Christ

We also need to make a conscious effort to exalt Christ in thought, word, and deed. Christ is the answer to the issues we have been addressing and the one who bridges so many doctrinal differences. Christ said, "And I, when I am lifted up from the earth, will draw all people to myself" (John 12:32 NRSV). This is true for the Christian as well as the non-Christian. When we exalt him and look to him, we will have less time and interest in scrutinizing others and being critical of them. Christ unites. Doctrine far too often divides, *unnecessarily divides.*

Paul gives us a good example of this in his letter to the Philippians. Though some were preaching Christ out of ulterior motives, he said, "So how am I to respond? I've decided that I really don't care about their motives, whether mixed, bad, or indifferent. Every time one of them opens his mouth, Christ is proclaimed, so I just cheer them on!" (Philippians 1:18 MSG). Once the disciples were confronted with a situation similar to Paul's, and John said, " 'Master...we saw a man driving out demons in your name and we tried to stop him, because he is not one of us.' 'Do not stop him,' Jesus said, 'for whoever is not against you is for you' " (Luke 9:49-50 NIV). Notice that Jesus did not say whoever is not with you is against you; on the contrary, whoever is not against you is for you. There is a big difference!

Love

The mark of a disciple is not the orthodoxy of doctrine, the amount of Bible knowledge possessed, or numerous other characteristics that we might name. Christ said the mark of his disciples is love for one another. He commands us to "love each other. Just as I have loved you, you should love each other" (John 13:34 NLT). The next verse *does not* say: "By this all men will know that you are My disciples, *if you hold to correct doctrine.*" Rather it says: "By this all men will know that you are my disciples, *if you love one another*" (John 13:35 NIV). Notice that these verses do not limit the ones we love to those who hold the same doctrinal positions that we uphold. Rather, Christ calls us to love all those who—fallible as they may be—like you and I, are endeavoring to follow Christ.

How Close to God's Throne?

John Wesley and George Whitefield were two great English evangelists who disagreed sharply on some doctrinal matters.

Once someone asked Wesley if he expected to see Whitefield in heaven. He said no. The questioner then responded, "Then you do not think Whitefield is a converted man?" To which Wesley is reported to have said: "Of course he is a converted man! But I do not expect to see him in heaven—because he will be so close to the throne of God and I so far away that I will not be able to see him!"[13]

If we can hold our theological convictions, yet sincerely affirm brothers and sisters with whom we differ, we are not likely to be stuck as an "Expert Christian." We need to fully appreciate that there may well be individuals in our lives whom we think are not as doctrinally "correct" as we think we are, yet we won't see them in heaven because they will be so far in front of us. The whole of Scripture certainly teaches that we should hold firmly to the truths of God, but that must never interfere with the higher priority on loving and trusting the God of all truth and genuinely loving all of his children.

You May Be Stuck as an "Expert Christian" If...

1. When you see or think of individuals you immediately tend to categorize them into a "we or them" doctrinal camp.

2. You hold truths about the Bible and Christ more important than your romance with Christ.

3. You have a great need to straighten people out who see things differently than you do.

4. Doctrinal correctness is of paramount importance.

Discussion Questions

1. Is there that much difference between knowing the God of all truth and knowing the truth about God?

2. Do you think too little as well as too much doctrine can create major problems for an individual or fellowship?

3. Are you and others in your association free to express their differences, doubts, or questions about doctrine without reprisal?

4. Do you think Christianity is known more for its love or contentiousness inside and outside the church?

5. To what extent do you think our personal need to be "right" plays into our defending "right" doctrine?

6. A.W. Tozer says "there is a difference between being Bible taught and being Spirit taught."[14] Do you agree? What is the difference?

Experiencing God's Love and Grace This Week

I am going to suggest something that is very hard for people prone to study the Scriptures in a utilitarian and cognitive manner. It is easy to read the Scriptures for knowledge and miss God's love and grace. The Benedictine monks of the fifth century were very aware of this and desired to read God's Word so that it touched their hearts. This was called *Lectio Divina*, literally "divine reading." This is devotional reading that seeks to hear what God wants to say to you and me today, rather than focusing on an intellectual understanding of the text. It is reading the Scriptures so that it will be *formational* rather than just *informational*. It is engagement with God at the depth of our beings. It is setting aside our own agendas and allowing God to speak to our hearts.

To do this we need to be in a comfortable, relaxed, unhurried environment, dismissing the world around us and the pressures of the day. We'll read a passage slowly, possibly several times, maybe even out loud, and then be quiet. Try and be conscious of God's loving presence. Focus on a word or phrase or several verses that the Holy Spirit highlights for you. Meditate on those passages. Be open to what God is saying to you about those portions of Scripture.

Try this several times this next week. If you don't know where to start, consider Psalm 23 one day, Psalm 100 or Exodus 15:1-18 another day.

4

The Grace-Abuser Christian

Dr. Johnson is a family practitioner. Early in his marriage, he and his wife were very dedicated Christians involved in Bible studies, small groups, and active in the college ministry at church. In more recent years, he has worked long, hard hours both in medical school and in developing his practice. In the process, his wife has had to make a life of her own. She has become deeply involved with the kids and their youth program at church. As the Johnsons have drifted apart, he has become closer to his front office manager, with whom he is in close contact 30 or more hours a week. Dr. Johnson tells me that he and his wife "have nothing in common," and that he is going to divorce her and marry his office manager.

Among other things, I asked him about his Christian commitment to marriage and how he thinks God will look on such a change. I can still remember him sitting in one of my office chairs, saying with a bold face that he would get divorced, remarried, and then ask God's forgiveness. And he added: "You know, we have a forgiving God." I was stunned at the callous and calculating nature of his comment. I don't know if my jaw dropped or not, but for a long moment I wasn't sure how to respond to him. Finally I asked, "Do you think we can abuse the grace and forgiveness of God?"

He retorted that he didn't think he was abusing God's grace. I cautioned him about being cavalier about God's grace saying, "I am not sure how God handles such situations." He clearly did not like my response and promptly dropped out of therapy. I am told that his interest in spiritual things is "almost nonexistent" now.

Abusing grace takes many forms. In the introductory chapter "Stalled on the Journey," I told you about Sheryl, who continued to be active in the Christian community by teaching a Bible study, among other things. She certainly didn't have any of the problems of the "Dutiful," "Corporate," or "Expert" Christians discussed earlier, for she had discovered God's grace—or at least that is what she called it. She was delighted to be free from the dogma and legalistic "to do" lists. She was enjoying her Christian life more than ever. She "found grace."

The very heart of the gospel—the good news—is grace. God's grace allows us to initially come to him, not on our merits, but on Christ's. God's grace allows us to remain in relationship with him despite the fact that we are imperfect people. Properly appreciated, grace is truly the antidote for so many problems in life and particularly for a person stuck in Stage 2—knowing God's truth and doing it. The more we understand God's marvelous grace and properly exercise it—an extremely important pursuit—the more grace-filled people we will be. The more grace-filled we are, the more God will be glorified. There's no such thing as too much grace! But grace can be misunderstood and inappropriately applied. Unfortunately, misconceptions about grace abound.

Misunderstanding Grace

We misconstrue grace for many different reasons. One problem that permeates evangelical Christendom since Martin

Luther is the fear of anything that might emphasize works. Thus we are highly sensitized to protect the doctrine of being saved by "faith alone." Anything that could be misunderstood as "works" is soundly condemned. In the process, we often distort an intricate and important relationship between grace and our efforts. Portions of the book of Romans and the entire epistles of Galatians and James were written to deal with this problem. Those who get stuck in Stage 2 can find many aspects of grace threatening— especially distortions of grace, so they often respond against perceived abuses of grace with an overreaction against grace.

Reactionary Grace

In contrast, people growing spiritually discover *grace as the way of living* the Christian life. Experiencing grace can occur any place on our journey. Discovering God's grace is often an exhilarating, life-changing, "aha" experience. How liberating to realize that we are not under the bondage of the law! God is not an efficiency expert in heaven with a clipboard in hand checking off whether we had a quiet time, prayed, witnessed, helped out at church, and so on. It is a momentous discovery to genuinely taste the goodness of "the God of all grace" (1 Peter 5:10). However, this can also be distorted, and a person can become a "Grace-Abuser." These individuals *react* to harsh Christianity and legalism and end up distorting the true nature of God's wondrous grace. Let's look at some of the ways this can happen.

Free from the Law?

One alteration of grace is antinomianism. *Anti* means "against" and *nomos* means "law." Thus, antinomianism is the belief that a person who is a Christian is freed from the moral law by virtue of grace. Romans 7:4 says, "You also were made to die to the Law through the body of Christ, so that you might be joined to another, to Him who was raised from the dead." Some conclude from verses like this that "we have died to the rules system. The law still exists, but it isn't intended for those of us who have received the righteous nature of Jesus Christ....We have no relationship to rules."[1] Another Christian leader puts it this way,

> What does it mean in everyday life to be delivered from the Law? At risk of a little overstatement I reply: It means that from henceforth I am going to do nothing whatever for God; I am never again going to try to please him. "What a doctrine!"...I jumped up and said: "Lord, are you really making no demands on me? Then I need do nothing more for You!"[2]

These statements come from very respected Christian leaders who probably would deny endorsing antinomianism—but to me, these particular quotes come very close. The person holding an antinomian position believes that since Christ did away with gaining access to God by the Old Testament Law, no laws are in effect for the Christian. In other words, grace covers everything.

A corollary of this position is "Christ plus nothing." The idea often expressed here is that I can do nothing to gain or add to my salvation. This is certainly true. But then people who espouse this position often go on to conclude that our efforts can do nothing and God doesn't expect us to do anything for the kingdom of God. It is true that God does not want any of our efforts that are the result of the flesh—they contribute nothing (Philippians 3:7-8). It is also valid that in our walk with God we are totally dependent on him. But he does want us to live a life of faith that inevitably will result in an "obedience of faith" (Romans 1:5; 16:26). In that sense God *does* want something from us.

Then there is the wonderful truth that Christ paid the price for our sins once and for all: past present, and future. Christ, at one point in human history, did take upon himself the sins of the whole world—past, present, and future. On this basis some people promote the doctrine that we don't need to ask for forgiveness, for the Christian has already been forgiven. Pressed to its logical conclusion, this means that we don't have to "repent" to be "saved." This proposition contradicts numerous passages in the Scriptures, such as 1 John 1:8-9: "If we say that we have no sin, we are deceiving ourselves and the truth is not in us. If we confess our sins, He is faithful and righteous to forgive us our sins and to cleanse us from all unrighteousness."

In addition, most Christian leaders who hold this theology typically minimize or negate any accounting that we Christians will face after we die. In fact, answering to God for our lives is a very unpopular subject today in most of Christendom! Yet it is one that the Scriptures clearly teach. The parable of the talents teaches the importance of making good use of what God has entrusted to us (Matthew 25:14-30). And 1 Corinthians 3:10-15 explicitly says that the quality of the work we do as Christians will be judged and rewarded appropriately.

The fact that we will give an accounting of our lives can be used as a horrible club, which is certainly not my intent. But, likewise, I don't think it should be ignored. Tozer comments: "The judgment unto death and hell lies behind the Christian, but the judgment seat of Christ lies ahead."[3] John Piper adds: "Both Jesus and Paul teach that believers will receive differing rewards in accord with the degree that their faith expresses itself in acts of service and love and righteousness."[4]

In summary we might say that our Western culture has a considerable emphasis toward antinomianism—that sinning is not really sinning at all. Unfortunately the church has also been influenced by such a culture.

Universalism

Some "Grace-Abusers" promote universalism. While rare for individuals in the evangelical camp to slip into universalism, some occasionally do. Universalism takes the doctrine of grace and pushes it to the point that says everyone in the world will ultimately be a recipient of that grace: Because Christ died for all, and God desires all to be saved, ultimately God will see that everyone is saved and no one will go to hell. For instance, one pastor writes:

> God has declared a blanket *presumption of innocence* over every one of us—a presumption based on the fact that he has gone ahead and made us innocent already in his Beloved Son....
>
> He says he's come not to judge but to save. He says not that he's going to deal with guilt but that because of what he's done, there just isn't any guilt left....
>
> God is simply not the infinite guilt-monger we've made him out to be. He's called off the whole guilt game for lack of interest on his part...even if you murdered....*God just isn't keeping score.* He's absolved Hitler; he's absolved all the child molesters and wife beaters in history; and he's absolved all of us before, during, and after our sins—in advance, free of charge, and forever.[5]

Putting "Grace-Abusers" into Perspective

Antinomianism and universalism are usually reactions to legalism. We find evidence early in the New Testament church of this same conflict. Judaizers were trying to coerce new Christians to follow the Law. Antinomians, who had discovered grace, were encouraging license. Paul, seeing the error in both extremes, tried to warn his readers about the dangers.

"Grace-Abusers" are promoting license—the "freedom" to do anything. License is not grace at all—it is an imitation of grace. Grace, of necessity, has limits. Allowing a four-year-old to run freely, including into the street, is not gracious. It is freedom and license, but it is not grace. Grace without limits is license. God is the author of grace but not license. Paul says: "You know well enough from your own experience that there are some acts of so-called freedom that destroy freedom" (Romans 6:16 MSG).

John Piper, addressing the distortions of grace, says:

> I have found that some popular notions of grace are so skewed and so pervasive that certain biblical teachings are almost impossible to communicate. For example, the biblical concept of unmerited, *conditional* grace is nearly unintelligible to many contemporary Christians who assume that *unconditionality* is the essence of all grace.
>
> To be sure, there is unconditional grace. And it is the glorious foundation of all else in the Christian life. But there is also *conditional* grace. For most people who breathe the popular air of grace and compassion today, *conditional grace* sounds like an oxymoron—like heavy feathers....I find the biblical thinking behind these kinds of conditional promises is uncommon in the minds of Christians today.[6]

We can see the application of conditional grace in relation to our eternal destiny. Christ died for the sins of the entire world—but to be the benefactor of that salvation, we must be willing to receive it. In other words, it is with the condition that we accept it. To deny conditional grace is to be a universalist.

The Works-Grace Paradigm

I have some Christian buddies, companions on the journey, I love. We delight to dialog about things of the Lord. Sometimes we get into some heated discussions. No matter if we agree on all the details or not, we share an underlying love and trust that surpasses any differences. Recently I got into a debate with one of the friends on the relationship between works and grace. He made a statement that sounded alarmingly close to antinomianism. I vehemently said, "We need balance between works and grace." He said, "*Balance* is not the right word." I hesitated, then stopped. After a moment I said, "You know, you are right. *Balance* is not the right word." The answer to the works versus grace conflict is not 50 percent works and 50 percent grace. Nor is it 10 percent works and 90 percent grace. Likewise it is not 90 percent works and 10 percent grace. Somehow, any such division totally misses the mark. If we only look at works and grace in a one-dimensional paradigm we are missing something.

Let me explain this with the "Spectrum of Works, Grace, & License" diagram. As one moves to the left in *Illustration 1a,* the amount of work one does increases, which I depict by the thickness of the arrow. As one moves to the right there is increasing grace up to a point and further movement to the right is a distorted form of grace, which I am calling license (sometimes referred to as "cheap grace"). But notice that I have placed license on a different level than grace because grace and license are very different from each other.

The Spectrum of Works, Grace, & License

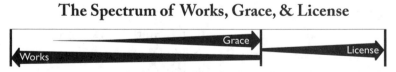

Illustration 1a

Now we can depict legalism and judgmentalism toward the left and antinomianism and universalism toward the right, as shown in *Illustration 1b.* You will note several other facets about the arrows depicting Grace, License, and Works. There is very little or no grace in judgmentalism; in legalism, there is a little more grace, but not much. Grace increases greatly in the middle third of the diagram. When you go further to the right, you get into increasing license.

The Spectrum of Works, Grace, & License

Illustration 1b

You will find the arrow depicting works only under the left two-thirds of the illustration since people promoting antinomianism and universalism generally oppose all works. But note that there is moderate work in the middle third of the diagram, the area in which God would have us function. As you move further to the left, the workload greatly increases and grace decreases. This leads to a weary Christian life.

As an aside, let me mention the nature of the work that I am talking about in the middle third of this diagram. It is not the clenched fist work of duty, earning, or rules. It is the *outflow* of a life of trust and love that we will discuss extensively in later chapters. As Dallas Willard often says, "Grace is not opposed to effort; it is opposed to earning."

I believe God wants us to live in the middle third of these diagrams. But *where* in the middle third? Is this place fixed or will it vary from time to time? It seems to me that it does vary, depending on numerous factors. But then how do we know how much grace and how much works? If we try to figure this out, even with the Scriptures, we are going to get it wrong! A "balance" between works and grace won't work either.

The Vertical Dimension Provides the Solution

The only way we will make any progress on these issues is to add a vertical dimension. We must look to Christ and the leading of the Holy Spirit in conjunction with the Word of God if we are going to get any resolution on this matter. Anything less will leave us self-centered, works-centered, or maybe Bible-centered, whereas we need to be Christ-centered. Every human effort to rationally determine the right "amount" of works and grace remains human effort—and it will come up short. We need the divine vertical dimension, which I have indicated in *Illustration 1c.*

The Spectrum of Works, Grace, & License

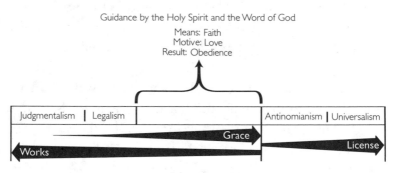

Illustration 1c

The means to activate this dimension is faith, the motive is love, and the enabler is the Holy Spirit. We cannot get it right unless all three of these ingredients are present. We can know the Scriptures from cover to cover and have the wisdom of Solomon, but we will not know how to apply the grace of God and act appropriately apart from the personal guidance of the Holy Spirit

(Galatians 5:18). Rules and guidelines, in the final analysis, will never transform the heart without the personal enlightenment of the Holy Spirit. This is the mistake the religious leaders of Christ's time made. Strictly following the written rules would have required Christ to endorse the stoning of the woman taken in adultery. The Pharisees got it wrong by following the black-and-white commands of God's written Word because they failed to listen to God's Spirit illuminating them on how, when, and where to apply his word.

We Are Dead to the System of Rules

"The Law" is the system of rules elaborated on in the Old Testament to make people aware of their sin and to point the way to a right relationship with God. Fortunately, that system has been abolished because it was always inadequate in itself and was intended to bring people to their crucial need of a trusting relationship in Christ. In one sense it can be rightfully said that we have "no relationship to rules," that we have been delivered from the law. God doesn't want us to *focus* on rules but on a person— Jesus Christ.

Under the New Covenant, our focus is on the person in whom we can trust—Christ (Romans 8:2). Just as keeping rules is not the focus, sin management (a close parallel) or any "marker" of spiritual success won't be the focus either. Trusting Christ will be the center of our attention. In the process we will probably find ourselves doing many of the things the rule keepers are doing— but with a different motivation and means. The *focus* won't be on trying to keep the rules; it will be on Christ. We will then be living by the "law of faith" (Romans 3:27,31) or as James puts it "the law of liberty" (James 1:25; 2:12).

Romans 6–8 uses the analogy that we are dead to the old marriage partner—rules—but alive and married to Christ. Paul elaborates: "You are no longer 'married to the law,' and it has no more control over you....[You] are a new person. And now you are 'married,' so to speak, to the one who rose from the dead....Now you can really serve God; not in the old way, mechanically obeying a set of rules, but in the new way, [with all of your hearts and minds]" (Romans 7:4,6 TLB, brackets in original).

The focal point must cease to be on rules and be put on trusting Jesus. Such a trust relationship with Christ will inevitably result in the *by-product* of pleasing him. Incidentally, we will note that we are in fact following many "rules" spelled out in the Scriptures.

The person prone to legalism will quickly object to "*many* rules" and say it should be "*all* the rules." I am aware that any qualification is highly disturbing to the black-and-white mind-set of some people who are prone to follow rules. Iron-clad rules seem safer, but following rules without the Holy Spirit's enlightenment and genuine love will snuff the spiritual vitality right out of the rule-keeper and his or her followers. It will inevitably lead to the inappropriate application of seemingly clear-cut black-and-white rules and damage, if not destroy, people...people whom Christ loves.

Remember, Christ didn't keep all the rules as understood by the religionists of his day. I am not saying this as a loophole to avoid any commandment or to water down the Scriptures, but to help you see that trusting Christ, being united with him, enables you to know when and how to apply which rules. Without the personal inspiration of the Holy Spirit we will never get this right.

All of this leads to the age-old question: "Does this mean that now we can go ahead and sin and not worry about it?" Which was rejoined with "Of course not!" (Romans 6:15 TLB). Properly applied grace leads to joyous freedom in Christ, not license.

The crux of the matter is: the focal point, Christ; the motive, love; and the means, trust. The *focus* will not be rules or, for that matter, obedience, which tends to put the attention right back on rules. It will be faith focused on Christ that will result in the "obedience of faith" (Romans 1:5; 16:26).

What's Our New Marriage Like?

Let me illustrate our new relationship with Christ relative to some old rules. We'll start with adultery. If my focal point is on sexual abstinence, I am married to a system of rules, which is the unsatisfactory Old Testament way of trying to please God. I may or may not be successful in maintaining abstinence. However, if under the New Covenant I am married to Christ, have a loving trust relationship with him, I will be aware that to consider adultery is an affront to him, so I won't even want to entertain such a thought. Therefore, I will be living a life consistent with this rule, not because I am focused on keeping the rule, but because my focus is on Christ, which will result in my not committing adultery.

Actually, we have a higher standard—a standard of the heart, not of actions (Matthew 5:20). Of course, if God has a person's heart, the appropriate actions will certainly follow. This is exactly what Christ told the legalists of his day; he focused on the *attitude* of their hearts, which in our current discussion was lust (Matthew 5:28). The follower of Christ will not focus on not committing adultery (which is still on the books according to, for example, Matthew 5:17; Romans 13:9; Revelation 2:22), but will center on Christ. Therefore, he or she won't even want *to want* to commit adultery. It will be anathema because of the love relationship with Christ. But the basis is not the law "thou shalt not commit adultery" or even "thou shalt not lust." It will be trust and love for Christ, *resulting* in obedience.

"Grace-Abusers" strongly proclaim that God has done away with the Law, but they often fail to emphasize the new, higher standard of the heart and spirit. On the other hand, those prone to focus on laws will be uncomfortable with much of what I have just said and may even take what I have said in this section and try to make a higher—impossible—law out of it. Either side can distort the truths of grace. To remain properly focused, we are utterly dependent upon the Holy Spirit to enable us to understand and live out the wonderful life of God's grace.

Let me illustrate our relationship with Christ to another "rule"—giving to the Lord's work. Ask any group of Christians how much a person should give to the Lord's work and the typical response is "ten percent." This comes from the law. There is an ample basis for this in the Old Testament, but what does the New Testament teach? Second Corinthians says, "So let each one give as he purposes in his heart, not grudgingly or of necessity; for God loves a cheerful giver" (9:7 NKJV). I suspect it delights the heart of God more if we give five percent to God's work when motivated by the Holy Spirit and a joyful heart than giving ten percent out of duty. But let me quickly add that when we are motivated by an overflowing heart of gratitude and led by his Spirit, God will touch hearts and many will find themselves joyfully giving much more than they would under any system of laws. Our focus will be on being sensitive to the Holy Spirit and the many needs around us, not on the financial ledger.

One final example of being led by the Spirit rather than by rules is with a quiet time. In chapter 1 I illustrated my drivenness to have a daily quiet time—a time in the morning to be with God. When I succeeded, I felt good; when I failed, it could wreck the rest of the day. In the last several decades, the compulsiveness is gone. Do I usually have a quiet time? Yes. Is it more meaningful? Often. When I miss do I feel guilty? Seldom. I only feel guilty when I could have had time with God and ignored the Spirit's leading. But as soon as I am aware of it, I try and own it and go on.

Can what I am saying about grace be abused? *Absolutely.* But apparently God so strongly wanted us to be the recipients of his grace that he was willing to risk it.

> So Christ has really set us free. Now make sure that you stay free, and don't get tied up again in slavery to the law....For you have been called to live in freedom—not freedom to satisfy your sinful nature, but freedom to serve one another in love (Galatians 5:1,13 NLT).

The question is whether we—as Christians—are willing to tolerate and promote such freedom in Christ?

Maturity Is Not Simple

Having said all of this, is there a time and place to teach rules? The answer is unequivocally yes. It is incumbent upon us to teach the teenager that God's sexual standard for the unmarried is abstinence. When we are beginning with Christ, some guidelines for growth are necessary and appropriate. You teach a child never to go into the street; as an adult you have to go into the street but you learn how, when, and where. Hopefully, we will become mature in Christ, learning how to fully embrace God's wonderful grace, without abusing it.

You May Be Stuck as a "Grace-Abuser" If...

1. You negatively react against rules, guidelines, or recommendations.

2. You minimize sin in the world at large and in the Christian in particular.

3. You believe Christians will not give an account of themselves before God.

4. You aren't concerned about the "lost."

Discussion Questions

1. How did your "divine reading," *Lectio Divina,* experience of reading God's Word work out for you this last week? Share your experience.

2. Do you agree that "ignorance and misconception about grace abound"? Give some examples.

3. What do you think of the theology "Christ plus nothing"? In what way is this a true statement, and how might it mislead?

4. To what extent do the people you associate with foster a legalistic or antinomian culture?

5. How do you understand the concept of being dead to the law and "married" to Christ?

6. The author illustrates our new relationship to rules using adultery, giving to God's work, and quiet time. What is your reaction to his description of the relationship to these

"rules" under the New Covenant? Take some other "rules" and describe how the New Covenant might apply to them.

7. Does a person have to go through a legalistic phase to really experience God's grace? Why or why not?

Experiencing God's Love and Grace This Week

Slowly read through chapters six through eight of the book of Romans daily, using different translations each time you read it. As you read, ask the Lord if there are some truths that he wants you to be aware of. Thank him that you are not under "the Law" and that there is no condemnation in Christ Jesus.

The Resistant Christian

God has disappointed a lot of people—both believers and nonbelievers alike. Patrick, a 43-year-old computer repairperson is clearly disappointed with God. In fact, he expresses downright anger at God. He tells me about growing up with a very caring, Christian mother and a "bum of a father who was never there." Patrick made a decision for Christ when he was eight years old. He became very active in the youth program at church and the Christian club on campus. When he was 17, his mother was rushed to the emergency room with a ruptured appendix. In surgery something went dreadfully wrong, and she never regained consciousness. Patrick kicks himself for not suing the doctors for malpractice before the statute of limitations ran out. He hasn't darkened the door of a church since his mother's funeral. He is furious with God. Patrick blames most of the world's ills on religion. At every opportunity, he launches into an attack on the bigotry of Christians. Patrick had a crisis of faith. He expected God to be a genie—and he didn't come through. There are a lot of Patricks in the world today, but you won't find them in church.

Crises of Faith

Crises affect all of us. They impact our faith in sundry ways. The Patricks in life are easy to recognize as they spew out their anger. However, there are large numbers of Christians sitting in our churches and reading books like this that have faced a crisis and resisted God in the process. This resistance can manifest itself in many different ways, but one common form is disappointment with God. Many times this will never be put into words, but that's the essence of it. Maybe the cause is an unfulfilled marriage, the loss of a promotion, infertility, the premature death of a loved one, or a chronic illness. Actually the list can be infinitely long. When these disappointed people fail to yield their lives and circumstances to God, they become "Resistant Christians." Their anger is sublimated into somewhat more acceptable forms such as bitterness, resentment, or criticism that can be expressed toward anyone—spouse, church, pastor, government, a political party, or a boss. Their bitterness may be camouflaged in all sorts of ways, including a saccharin-sweet variety. Because one is dealing with a problem of the heart, the potential manifestations are legion.

So What Makes Us Disappointed with God?

Expecting the Wrong Things from God

We have all heard about the prosperity gospel—God supposedly promising everyone health and wealth. Most evangelical Christians don't think this "gospel" is an accurate representation of the Scriptures, but I suggest to you that most of us, deep within, expect things from God that he hasn't promised, such as reasonably good health, a steady job, food, and security.

My friend Lloyd comes to mind. He is very active at church, has gone on a number of short-term mission trips, and generously supports missionaries. His life was going great until he faced a crisis of faith—his daughter was born with spina bifida. Once Lloyd confided in me that "if I live a good Christian life, I expect God will keep my family from all catastrophic problems." Now

God has "broken his part of the bargain," and Lloyd is disappointed with God. Lloyd continues to sing God's praises each Sunday, but he is often critical of the pastor and church.

God isn't a Coke dispenser. We all have had run-ins with vending machines that don't keep their part of the bargain. We put a dollar in the money slot and expect a Coke to drop in the shelf below. Instead, nothing happens. We push the "coin return" and still nothing happens. I don't know about you, but I can sense the surge of adrenalin with feelings of anger because "I've been gypped." I am prone to bang on the dispenser, just a little, in hopes of getting my Coke or money back. What happened? I entered into a bargain with the vending machine: "I'll meet your advertised price, and you will give me a Coke." I met my part of the bargain, and when the machine doesn't fulfill its part, I'm angry. The same dynamics occur in a lot of situations in life. Many times we aren't even aware that we have entered into these contracts until they are violated.

Lloyd expected God would keep him and his family from any catastrophic problem if he lived a "good" Christian life. He was trying *to earn God's favor* and expected God to deliver the desired outcome. But this was a one-way contract! God never signed it. We get into all kinds of trouble when we expect things from God that he's never promised. Crises are the very thing that God will use to reveal these unilateral contracts. If, in your heart of hearts, you are hurt, bitter, angry, or disappointed with God or *life,* you may be a "Resistant Christian."

Who's God?

Another cause of the "Resistant Christian" is control. When we demand to control our lives we immediately buck heads with God. We are placing ourselves in the role of God—and God won't allow it. Sin is really independence from God—"I'll do it my way, thank you!"

As with the rich young ruler, God will ask some things of us that will make it exceedingly clear where our hearts are and who is in control of our lives. Jesus said, "Anyone who intends to come with me has to let me lead. You're not in the driver's seat; I am" (Matthew 16:24-26 MSG). A.W. Tozer says:

> Let a man set his heart only on doing the will of God and he is instantly free....It is only when we introduce our own will into our relation to God that we get into trouble....Then I'll begin to blame whoever stands in my way and excuse my spiritual breakdowns as being caused by someone or something that is working to "hinder" me....If we find ourselves irked by external hindrances, be sure we are victims of our own self-will. Nothing can hinder the heart that is fully surrendered and quietly trusting...God.[1]

Crises Reveal the Heart

When we face a crisis a highly held belief is challenged. We either yield or resist. When we resist, our egos get wrapped up in the issue, especially when we are trying to defend our reputations. We often come out fighting, cloaking our reaction as a defense for "God's work"—or so we tell others and ourselves. We need to be very careful here, as it may actually be the big "I" fighting for, and by, the flesh.

We all know of prominent Christian leaders who have gotten into trouble, typically in sexual or financial indiscretions. It seems that more often than not, they fight for their reputation and "ministry," often not fully following the recommendations of those overseeing their rehabilitation. Then, at best, they limp along the rest of their lives. This is more tragic than the original transgression. Such persons fail at the point of deep repentance and thus fall short of being men and women after God's own heart. Their conduct more closely resembles the "yes, buts" of King Saul's superficial repentance.

Our response to crises and disappointments reveals the motives of our hearts. It reveals idolatry, pride, and the intent of our inner life probably more quickly than anything else. If, in our heart of hearts, there is anything more important than God, our response to crises will manifest it. When Christ is truly Lord of our lives and we have humble hearts, crises will not interrupt our walk of faith. The apostle Paul is a good example of this. And the supreme model is the Lord, who willingly allowed himself to be falsely accused, tortured, and crucified without ever defending himself. In the final analysis, crises reveal who is Lord of our lives—the big "I" or Christ.

The Test

Christ told us we would go through difficult times and the crucial test is whether we are willing to continually be joyful *in Christ*. This admittedly is a tall order. But the fact is, a lack of joy often reveals a "Resistant Christian." James says, "Consider it all joy, my brethren, when you encounter various trials." *The Message* renders it, "Consider it a sheer gift, friends, when tests and challenges come at you from all sides. You know that under pressure, your faith-life is forced into the open and shows its true colors" (James 1:2-4).

The natural response when we are on the throne of our lives is anger and resentment toward things we don't like. When Christ is on the throne, bitterness and resentment will be replaced with an underlying sense of joy. That doesn't mean that everything will turn out in this life the way we would like. In fact, we may experience sorrow, which is not incompatible with joy.[2] (Furthermore, I don't mean to suggest that any of this is easy or an instantaneous process. We will discuss this further in chapter 12.)

Christ did not enjoy the suffering he went through, and he even *felt* abandoned by God! Nevertheless, he was ultimately able to be joyful (see Hebrews 12:1-3). Paul says, "In everything give thanks; for this is God's will for you in Christ Jesus" (1 Thessalonians 5:18). I don't think this means that what is bad is good; nor does it mean we should be thankful for what is evil. It means that in the midst of this sin-sick world, which includes personal disappointments, we need to be thankful to God for who he is and that he walks with us on our journey.

We can be assured that all our crises have passed through the sieve of his permissive will. Understanding and accepting this helps us to have an attitude of joy—joy because we are walking with the God of the universe, the one who understands all. Joy because through all eternity we will have abundant reasons to be joyful.

To Become Mature

James tells us that God *uses* these crises so that we might "become mature and well-developed, not deficient in any way" (James 1:4 MSG). Popular Christian author Phillip Keller wrote how such a crisis became a positive step in his walk with God. He said that as a result of his wife's cancer his

> chief preoccupation in life began to shift from one of self-interest and self-preoccupation to that of service for others. Not that this was not a desirable redirection, a good step, in my spiritual saga. The tragedy was that it *was not the best step.* It would take at least another ten or twelve years of tempestuous living…before at long last I would stumble onto

[the] eternal truth that we are not here either just for self or just for service but for the *Savior...to know God and to love Him.*[3]

It seems to me from this description that God used a crisis in Phillip Keller's life to move him from the self-interest of Stage 1 to the service of Stage 2—a positive growth step. But it took Mr. Keller another 10 or 12 years to experience greater maturity on his spiritual journey. Hopefully we can learn to turn the crises in our lives into stepping-stones for growth.

You May Be Stuck as a "Resistant Christian" If...

1. While reading this chapter some unfortunate situation or event came to mind with a sense of pain, ill feeling, disappointment, unforgiveness, resentment, or anger.

2. There is a person or place you don't want to encounter.

3. You find it difficult to rejoice and be thankful in Christ.

4. You feel disappointed with God or life.

5. You are unwilling to give total control of your life to Christ.

Discussion Questions

1. In your Christian community would it be O.K. to say you were disappointed with God? What kind of a response do you think you would get?

2. Are you disappointed with life? Have you ever been?

3. Can you give examples of crises where you either resisted or yielded to God's hand? What were the outcomes?

4. What is the most difficult circumstance or crisis you personally have dealt with?

5. When you use some kind of vending machine and it fails to fulfill its part of the bargain, how do you react? Is there a parallel with bigger disappointments in your life?

6. When you are hurt, angry, or resentful, do you think a "contract" or expectation is being violated? Think of the last time you were angry. What expectation was violated? Was the expectation valid?

7. Why do you think some people go through a horrendous crisis and blossom, while others get stuck?

Experiencing God's Love and Grace This Week

Consider praying Psalm 139 to God. Read each verse slowly. Meditate on it, and respond to it as the Holy Spirit leads. Be open to any old hurts or disappointments in life that aren't fully resolved. Ask God for his grace in looking at them and dealing with them. (If you don't have time for the whole chapter, consider verses 1-6 and 23-24). You may want to read chapter 1, "A Fatal Error," in Philip Yancey's *Disappointment with God: Three Questions No One Asks Aloud* (Grand Rapids, MI: Zondervan, 1988).

6

The Emotional Christian

Growing up on "the wrong side of the tracks," Todd frequently used alcohol and marijuana. He was in jail when he first heard of the claims of Christ. After he got out, he started attending a church where the emphasis was on experience. God became very real, and Todd's life changed radically. For several years he remained on a spiritual "high." But then the old feelings of emptiness returned. He occasionally numbed himself with drugs, feeling horribly guilty afterward. Church helped alleviate the emptiness, but it didn't last. He remained on a spiritual roller coaster until he realized he was stuck on an experiential relationship with God.

Todd had been strongly influenced by an *emotional form of spirituality.* This was helpful for a while, but he eventually found something was missing. He heard me speaking on the seven stages of spiritual growth and said, "Your Pyramid of Spiritual Growth implies that we all start at the bottom and work up. I started at the top and had to work down. I was introduced to Christ at a church where it was all about experience. That is what we were taught. I finally came to the awareness that I needed some grounding in the Scriptures. I had to go back and work on some of the basics of the Christian life."

His story illustrates several points. First, everyone is different. Each of us meets the Lord in our own unique way. Likewise, there are wide variations in our growth patterns. Todd's emotional emphasis illustrates what I am calling the "Emotional Christian" or the "Experientialist."

What do I mean by the "experientialist?" I am using this term to refer to those who are deeply involved in the experiential emphasis of Christianity to the exclusion of most other aspects that we have discussed—especially biblically based theology and "rational thinking." The experientialist relies primarily on his or her personal experience in spiritual matters. Feelings dominate. The mystic fits into this category. According to Webster, a mystic is "characterized by [the] esoteric, otherworldly....a state of spiritual ecstasy."[1] *Harpers Bible Dictionary* defines mystic as "one who attains direct knowledge of God and of spiritual truth through immediate intuition or spiritual insight. His experiences transcend those of the ordinary man."[2]

Many of the early church leaders, both male and female, were mystics, including some of the writers on the stages of growth. It is my opinion that if one gets *too far* into the experiential, especially moving into the mystical, spiritual growth becomes distorted. In fact, mysticism can take an extreme form, emphasizing direct intuition or illumination from God to the point of subordinating the authority of the Scriptures. This clearly opens the door to error regarding God and his truths.

On the other hand, if there is no mystery or emotionality in our walk with God, our relationship is pretty dry or even dead.

Holy Mysteries

The facts are—there is a lot of mystery in faith.[3] There are numerous mysteries in the Christian life, including the truths that

Christ is in us as believers and that God has given us new hearts. There is a lot about God and theology that we just don't fully understand. The person uncomfortable with "mystery" will try and explain everything, but if we are going to grow in Christ we must accept the fact that spiritual matters involve considerable unknowns.

Furthermore, a satisfying relationship with God includes a phenomenal interactive emotional relationship with him. Without that, our walk with God will be as dry as the ink on these pages. Deep within our hearts we all desire an ongoing, experiential relationship with God. He made us for that, and we are incomplete without it.

Why Individuals Become Experientialists

Why do some individuals take the experiential to the extreme? I believe there are four primary reasons. As a psychiatrist, I am very aware that one's innate personality plays a role in this issue. Genetics are significant. I am not saying anyone is genetically destined to be an experientialist, but some people have an increased propensity in that direction (others have just as strong a propensity in the opposite direction).

The second important reason is teaching. Remember Todd? He only had exposure to Christians with a strong bent toward the emotional side of spirituality.

The third reason is resistance to the more concrete activities typical of Stage 2—knowing God's truths and doing them. Such individuals don't want to be regimented in Bible study or in how they minister to the world around them.

Closely related to this is the fourth reason, which is "reaction formation." When we don't like something or think it is wrong or misleading, we may overreact to it and more vehemently embrace the opposite side of the issue. This is reaction formation. We are oftentimes unaware of the extent of our overreaction. Since this is such an important phenomenon both in life in general and in the Christian community, let me elaborate. All of us, to various degrees, slip into reaction formation from time to time. Satan takes advantage of this tendency and uses it to his own ends, often turning Christian against Christian.

People tend to migrate toward extremes on issues. This tendency, according to C.S. Lewis, often leads us to debating each side:

> Which of these two errors is the worse. That is the devil getting at us. He always sends errors into the world in pairs—pairs of opposites. And he always encourages us to spend a lot of time thinking [about] which is worse. You see why, of course? He relies on your extra dislike of the one error to draw you gradually into the opposite one. But do not let us be fooled. We have to keep our eyes on the goal and go straight through between both errors.[4]

Thus, individuals "reacting" to a rational, black-and-white, concrete form of Christianity may compensate by going to the other extreme—the experiential.

The Rationalist vs. the Experientialist

The Rationalist is typically the individual deeply immersed in knowing God's truths. He often detests mystery, especially anything approaching the mystical or "touchy-feely" emotionality. He is much more comfortable living in a black-and-white world, abhorring shades of gray.

The Experientialist has been freed from black-and-white answers and programs of the persons who overemphasize cognitively knowing God's truth. He relishes living with less rigid answers. He is absorbed with feeling and experience, and that is the platform from which he operates.

The Rational–Experiential Triangle

Baron von Hugel, in *Mystical Element of Religion,* describes a tension that exists between three groups of people.[5] The first group is the Historical/Institutional; the second is the Intellectual/Scientific. I place these two groups in the "Rational" category. The third group is the Mystical/Emotional—the "Experiential" group. An individual who reacts against the rational is propelled toward experiential spirituality.

One way to conceptualize the phenomenon that we have been talking about is with "The Rational–Experiential Triangle" (see *Illustration 2a*). At the lower left corner is the Historical/Institutional, on the lower right is the Intellectual/Scientific, and at the top is the Mystical/Emotional.

The Rational–Experiential Triangle

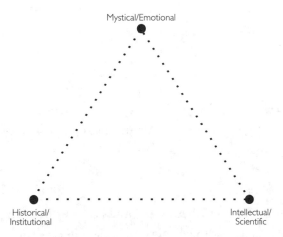

Illustration 2a

A person could be at any point within the dotted lines of the triangle. For the sake of illustration, if an individual relied equally on the Historical/Institutional and Intellectual/Scientific and had no propensity toward the Mystical/Emotional he would be at point "a" as shown in *Illustration 2b*. If a person had an equal propensity toward all three perspectives he or she would be right in the center of the triangle, as illustrated with point "b."

The Rational–Experiential Triangle

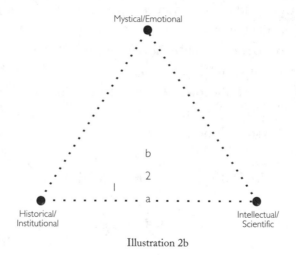

Illustration 2b

As I think of my own life I probably started out at point "1" and now would place myself at point "2." Each of us has a propensity to be at fairly precise points in this triangle at various times in his spiritual journey.

What's Ideal?

I cannot tell you where you should be on this triangle except to say that I suspect the ideal is someplace *around* the center, and getting too close to any corner is clearly unwise. In our approach, we must be grounded in the Word of God. We need a bedrock foundation of truth upon which to base our relationship with God. The Scriptures give us that bedrock and are an essential building block in our spiritual journey. On the other hand, *we desperately need and long for a dynamic, intimate, emotional relationship with our risen Lord*—an *experiential relationship* that necessarily involves mystery. It is not an "either or" situation; it is a "both and" situation.

I believe we need to learn as individuals and as a church to use our "right-brain" experientialist side and our "left-brain" rationalist side in *harmony* so that we don't function like a stroke victim but as a whole body. May God help each of us to appropriately hold on to our rational moorings while learning to experientially respond to God's fantastic personal interaction with us, *accepting* and *feeling* his phenomenal love and grace! This is mystery—but a wonderful mystery of personally walking in the presence of Christ.

You May Be Stuck as an "Emotional Christian" If...

1. You abhor regimentation.

2. Feelings tend to dominate your life.

3. You don't know the Bible really well.

4. You react to a rational approach to Christianity.

Discussion Questions

1. How has God impacted your life or made himself known to you this week?

2. Do you have an experiential relationship with God?

3. How do you feel about the mystery in the Christian life?

4. Give an example of your responding to an issue with reaction formation. How about a spiritual issue? Elaborate.

5. Draw a "Rational–Experiential Triangle" and mark the point on it that best describes where you were when you first began your spiritual journey. Now mark another point showing where you are today. Are you where you want to be?

6. Is there an ideal place for an individual to be on the "Rational–Experiential Triangle?"

Experiencing God's Love and Grace This Week

For the "experientialist" (in the upper half of the Rational–Experiential Triangle), get some time alone with God and your Bible and meditate on John 14:6; 8:31-32; 2 Timothy 3:12-17.

For the "rationalist" (in the lower half of the Rational–Experiential Triangle), I encourage you to get alone with God in his marvelous nature—away from everything man-made if you can. Pick the best place that is practical in your situation. Quiet yourself before God and his handiwork and ask him to help you appreciate him and the world he has made. Praise him for who he is and what he has created. Listen to what he says to you. It may be hard, but try not to be in a hurry. Spend at least 20 minutes in silent listening (see Psalm 46:10).

The Runt Christian

Early in my Christian life, when working with marines heading for the battlefields of Korea, a young marine, Jeff, came into the Servicemen's Center. An older, gray-haired Christian and I talked with him. The young marine told of a life of debauchery, but added that he had once "prayed the sinner's prayer." This was enough to trigger a sermon from the older Christian about "eternal security" and the fact that this questioning marine was "absolutely saved." But the question went through my mind, "How can he be so sure?" If the man wasn't saved, what kind of disservice was the gray-haired Christian doing him, trying to convince him he was actually saved? What if he was erroneously convinced he was saved, and in six weeks lay dead on a hillside in Korea? I never saw the marine again, and I don't know what happened to him—but the troubling question has remained in my mind.

A more recent example comes to mind. Randy was struggling with the "assurance of salvation." I tried to help him evaluate his eternal status based on Scripture, but the question never seemed to get clarified. Later I found out through another source that during the same time we were talking he was having several affairs.

These scenarios raise the question, "Who is a Christian, and what is saving faith?" In this chapter I would like to briefly address five situations: (1) the Nonbeliever, (2) the "Christian" Nonbeliever, (3) the Runt Christian, (4) the Believing Doubter, and (5) the Searchers. Individuals in these categories get stuck either just before or shortly after becoming true believers in Christ.

The Unsaved

Nonbelievers

Obviously, the nonbeliever has never been born into God's spiritual family so there has been no spiritual life or growth to be arrested. These people don't claim to be Christians. Some may be acutely aware of their spiritual plight, others are unaware of their spiritual deadness.

Stillborn Christians

Paul said, "I'm finding that not all 'believers' are believers" (2 Thessalonians 3:2 MSG). In other words, some who *profess* to be believers—Christians, born-again—really aren't. Such people think they are saved, but are not. One might even call them " 'Christian' Nonbelievers" or "Stillborn Christians." They may actually believe in Christ, and yet not have a saving belief.[1]

Some Christians have fostered stillborn believers in their zeal for the gospel and their fixation on converts as the bottom line. They seldom talk about repentance, remorse, regret, or anguish over sin. They often encourage no more than a mental assent—the kind of belief even the demons have (James 2:19-20). John Piper states, "The New Testament warning that some in the church 'shall not inherit the kingdom of God' (Galatians 5:21; 1 Corinthians 6:9) is stunning. It is astonishing to me how many Christians are blasé about this matter. It's as though salvation were a casual and obvious thing. It's as though grace were a catch-all for every kind of divine tolerance that anyone can imagine."[2] There are, in fact, some scary verses in the Scriptures:

> Not everyone who says to Me, "Lord, Lord," will enter the kingdom of heaven, but he who does the will of My Father who is in heaven will enter. Many will say to Me on that day, "Lord, Lord, did we not prophesy in Your name, and in Your name cast out demons, and in Your name perform many miracles?" And then I will declare to them, "I never knew you; depart from Me, you who practice lawlessness" (Matthew 7:21-23).

Immature Christians

Runt Christians

At one point when his disciples were just starting to grow in their faith, Jesus said to them, "You men of little faith" or as *The Message* so graphically portrays it, "Runt believers! Haven't you caught on yet?" (Matthew 16:8-9). Certainly God loves each one of us and wants the very best for us. It's not his desire that any of us remain infantile. But if we fail to drink of the milk of God's Word and grow, I am afraid we can become emaciated and ineffective.

Runt Believers could also be called "Decision Christians," "Dotted-Line Christians," or "Saved-as-by-Fire Christians." They are getting to heaven by the "skin of their teeth." Individuals in this category are, frankly, immature Christians. They may just have made a decision to receive Christ or they may have made their decision decades ago and are stuck. The writer of Hebrews addresses such people:

You have been Christians a long time now, and you ought to be teaching others. Instead, you need someone to teach you again the basic things a beginner must learn about the Scriptures. You are like babies who drink only milk and cannot eat solid food. And a person who is living on milk isn't very far along in the Christian life…Let us go on instead and become mature (Hebrews 5:12–6:1 NLT).

Believing Doubters

I am convinced that there are many dear Christian doubters. They are saved, but they worry that they aren't saved. They are true believers, but live their lives plagued with doubt and nagging uncertainties. These believers suffer in silence because their Christian brothers and sisters don't understand their struggle. If they share their anguish they get pat answers or, worse yet, condemnation. The person who has never had a sensitive conscience just doesn't comprehend the turmoil with which these individuals continually deal. So they have learned to keep their struggle to themselves…but then it festers.

In my experience, many of these sensitive individuals have been abused in childhood and, not infrequently, mistreated by harsh, guilt-inducing Christians. They are often guilt- and depression-prone people. "Believing doubters" are often well versed in their Bibles and work hard for the kingdom, but they still question their salvation.

Generally, believing doubters don't question the existence of God or even the truthfulness of the Scriptures. They doubt that they have believed "right," that they have enough faith, or that God could love them. You might call this person a self-doubter or a believer who lacks confidence.

My wife is a dedicated Christian. Many years ago she was the women's area director for a Christian organization and at one point was questioning her salvation. She went to a well-known Christian leader and verbalized her question. Knowing virtually nothing about her, he said, "It's conceivable that you have never been born again." These words and the way they were said, coming from such a respected authority in Christendom, devastated and troubled my wife for years. But the reality was that she did have a "saving faith," but it was overshadowed by doubts.

The Searchers

The authors of *The Critical Journey* describe a group of people they call "the searchers."[3] As I see this group, they are individuals who often have had a religious upbringing and may or may not have experienced genuine faith in Christ. Most have never met the authentic Christ. Many have experienced an abusive religious parent, pastor, or institutional church. They have thrown formal Christianity away, but they are ever searching for something to replace it. It might be through drugs, sex, materialism, groups such as AA, or new age experiences. They have rejected their caricature of Christ, but nothing else satisfies. You might say they are seeking what they are avoiding. Sometimes, if they can meet people living a life in Christ *without religious trappings,* they can get past the obstacles to experience Christ's magnificent life.

God Has So Much More for Us!

We have explored numerous specific obstacles to our spiritual growth—and in fact there are many others we don't have space for. Maybe you have never really started your journey or maybe you're a "babe" in Christ or possibly a dutiful and weary Christian. There is hope!

Be assured that God loves you! He extended his marvelous love, grace, and acceptance to the outcasts, prostitutes, and hated tax collectors of his day, and he wants to do the same to you and me—whoever we are and wherever we are on our journey.

In the next section we'll discuss the Seven Stages of Growth to becoming mature in Christ. We'll see if there is anything obstructing your moving from one stage to the next.

You May Be Stuck at the Point of Salvation If...

1. You have never, by faith, trusted the finished work of Christ for your eternal salvation.

2. You have never intentionally pursued your relationship with Christ.

3. You are plagued with doubts about your salvation.

4. You are searching for something you can't seem to find.

Discussion Questions

1. Describe your early religious experiences. Who influenced you? How did it make you feel and respond?

2. What do you think of the five categories of individuals at or around the stage of salvation? Are there any modifications you would make to these categories?

3. A.W. Tozer says: "To be saved appears to be the highest ambition of most Christians today. To have eternal life and know it is the highest aspiration of many. Here they begin and here they end."[4] What is your reaction to this statement?

4. Do you think there are many "believing doubters" in your fellowship? How would you know? How could you be helpful to them even if you don't know who they are?

5. Do you think people can excessively emphasize salvation by "faith only"?

6. How can you reach "the searchers" if religious trappings push them away?

Experiencing God's Love and Grace This Week

If you have any question about your eternal destiny, find a trustworthy Christian friend or pastor with whom you can talk about your spiritual birth and new life in Christ. Read John 3:16; 10:10; Romans 3:23; 6:23; 5:8; John 14:6; 1:12; Revelation 3:20; John 5:24; and 1 John 5:11-12. It is crucial that you get this matter resolved. If your relationship with Christ is settled, try and be cognizant this week of how great a salvation he has given you. As you think of this, express your thanks to him.

Part Two

The Road to Being Complete in Christ or Seven Stages to Spiritual Maturity

The life of faith is not a one-time experience, nor is it a destination. It's a journey.

God has a wonderful trip he wants to travel with us, and there are mileage markers along the way indicating our progress. How far have you traveled...and where do you go next?

Seven Stages to Spiritual Maturity

Stage 1
Getting the Right Start—
Starting the journey with Christ

Stage 2
Knowing and Doing—
Learning God's truths and doing them

Stage 3
The Authentic Heart—
Being what you profess

Stage 4
Experiencing God—
Developing an intimate relationship with God

Stage 5
The Crises of Faith—
Successfully navigating life's difficulties

Stage 6
The Exchanged Life—
Cultivating a deep trust and rest in Christ

Stage 7
The Life of Adoration—
Realizing and responding to God's profound love

8

Getting the Right Start

Stage 1: Starting the journey
with Christ

My wife and I had gone out for dinner with our neighbors, Steve and Linda. After a nice meal we came back to our house and visited until eleven o'clock. Eventually we started talking about spiritual things, and it turned out that Steve was a skeptic and Linda wasn't sure what she believed. In the course of our conversation, we mentioned the book *Daktar,* which tells of a physician's journey from being a skeptic to his confrontation with Christ.[1] Steve was intrigued, borrowed the book, and later told me that he "stayed up half the night reading the book." Several months later Steve began his new life in Christ.

Every Life Must Have a Beginning

When parents see their newborn infant for the first time, they usually study the child's features and count the tiny fingers and toes. Marveling at this complete little person and discovering that each limb has all five digits, they exclaim, "She's perfect!" All the parts are there and working properly for a new baby. Sometimes when the Bible talks about believers being "perfect," its meaning carries the same idea: God has supplied us with everything we need to be complete, whole, "perfect" Christians, even though at that point in time we have a lot of growing to do as we are just beginning our spiritual pilgrimage. Just as our physical life has a beginning—so too our spiritual life must have a beginning.

Salvation

I remember when I was nine years of age, peeking through the flaps of a large tent near home and hearing an evangelist describe in detail the anguishes of the fires of hell. It scared me to death and I left. In subsequent months I repeatedly went forward at a number of church services to receive the gift of eternal life. But because of doubt, it took six months before I had the *assurance* of salvation—a confidence that I would not experience the "lake of fire and brimstone." To this day I can remember leaving the little chapel feeling as though I were walking on clouds. There was a phenomenal sense of God's accepting love and forgiveness that I immediately shared with my family. The next day I took my little red Gospel of John and shared with a playmate what had happened.

The circumstances of people coming to Christ are as varied as we are. In the Scriptures no two individuals came to Jesus the same way. So it is with us—the situations surrounding our encounter with Christ are extremely different. Nevertheless, there are a few *essential* ingredients to having "saving faith."

The Nature of Saving Faith

So what is necessary for saving faith that results in the eternal salvation of our souls? First of all, there needs to be contrition of heart and awareness that we are sinners unable to save ourselves.[2] Second, by faith we need to accept that salvation that can come only through the finished work of Christ on the cross.[3] Third, we need to be very clear as to the nature of our faith in Christ. It is more than cognitive belief; it includes an actual trusting of ourselves to God.[4] Trust indicates a reliance on and a continual commitment to Jesus as the means to live our Christian life. This is saving faith.

Knowing You Are Saved Is Crucial

God not only wants you saved, he wants you to know it. In chapter 7 we discussed the "Believing Doubter"—the individual who is truly born again but struggles with doubts. Here are a few steps that will help a person solidify his or her confidence in being a child of God.

1. Please know that the Lord is very patient with sincere, struggling doubters. Many of the Old Testament patriarchs had times of doubt. Christ was kind to "Doubting Thomas" and showed him his scarred hands to prove he was the risen Christ. Even John the Baptist, whom Christ called the greatest born of women, had his doubts.

2. Realize the importance of a specific diagnosis as to the nature of the problem. Many different causes can underlie doubting—it is specific to your situation. The real problem may not be spiritual at all, but rather a physical or emotional issue: an endocrine disorder, depression, perfectionism, or chronic self-doubt based on childhood experiences. Or the difficulties may lie with faulty Christian teaching and unrealistic expectations, such as expecting temptations or troubles to just disappear.

3. Be sure that you have, at a specific point in your life, put your trust in the finished work of Christ. Then remember that the commitment of your life to God has been made. It is a done

decision, an act of the will. And it is not a work of yours that requires you to *feel* any particular way. Now it is in God's hands.

4. Consider whether there is any *specific* sin adversely affecting your relationship with God. If there is, confess and forsake it.

5. Be sure you are having some fairly regular time with the Lord in his Word and through prayer, as well as having the fellowship of other believers.

6. Seek out a mature, understanding Christian who will listen and assist you in working through the issues involved. In some instances, a mature, competent Christian counselor may be needed.

Tim is a conscientious 18-year-old high school senior who is struggling with many doubts. Foremost on his list is the question of whether or not God could love him and whether or not he is really "saved." He "accepted Christ" at camp when he was 11 years old, but he was never sure if he really meant it. His parents divorced when he was six, and over the next ten years he was shuttled between their homes. Tim was also suffering from clinical depression. With appropriate professional therapy his depression lifted after two months. Shortly thereafter he came into the office and said that he no longer doubted his salvation, and he was beginning to believe that God really did love him.

Guilt and doubts can be the result of depression. Sometimes depression comes as a result of sin—and then sin needs to be dealt with accordingly. However, not all depression is due to unconfessed sin of the sufferer. Such situations require that the specific cause be remedied.[5]

The most crucial aspect of life is that we objectively—from God's perspective—have made our peace with God. Hopefully our subjective feelings will catch up to the facts of our position in Christ. Further growth in Christ will be a tremendous help.

Moving On

Don't forget! God loves you wherever you are on your journey, and he wants a personal relationship with you! It is not his will that any should perish but that all come to the Father who, with outstretched arms is ready to embrace us. He wants to put a royal robe on you, a ring on your finger, and throw you a party. God wants you to be "saved," and to know it. He wants you to experience the greatest adventure in life—to become mature in Christ. For a believer not to grow would be as sad as the infant remaining in a crib the rest of his or her life. God has an exciting journey ahead for you.

The Pyramid of Spiritual Growth

To illustrate the stages of growth I will use layers that form a pyramid. You will notice that in *Illustration 3*, the first tier or foundational layer has been labeled "Salvation." It is upon this initial relationship with Christ that all the other stages will be built.

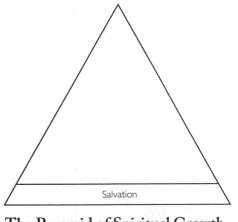

The Pyramid of Spiritual Growth

Illustration 3

Discussion Questions

1. How, when, and where did you first experience God in your life?

2. Have you experienced spiritual birth? Describe the circumstances and what happened in your life.

3. Do you think it is important to know the exact date you were saved?

4. Have you ever doubted your salvation? If so, how have you dealt with it?

5. Is it possible to have faith without doubt? Explain your answer.

Experiencing God's Love and Grace This Week

Read three chapters in the Gospel of John each day this week. Ask God through his Spirit to teach you the truths he would have you learn about your relationship with Christ. Look for what the Gospel teaches about initially coming into a relationship with Christ and how one abides in Christ and experiences the abundant life.

9

Knowing and Doing

Stage 2: Learning God's truths and practicing them

Tom, a marine corporal and rifle instructor at Camp Pendleton, was, you might say, a "Runt Christian." He had accepted Christ but had not grown in his faith. Then he met a gung-ho Christian on the base who brought him into the Serviceman's Center where he started to grow in Christ. Tom learned what God had to say to him through the Bible and did what it taught. This led to Bible school, college, and the pastorate. He continues to grow in his faith, careful to feed on God's Word and to practice all it teaches. God has used his life to touch many for the kingdom, including some who are on the mission field today. Tom continues to minister to his congregation in Pennsylvania.

Tom is a wonderful example of the fact that the new believer in Christ must mature in his faith to experience all the riches of God.

Knowing

Just as healthy babies born into the world need food to grow, so does the young Christian. We are exhorted: "Like newborn babies, crave pure spiritual milk, so that by it you may grow up in your salvation" (1 Peter 2:2 NIV). The primary nutrient for the new Christian is God's Word, the Bible. If we want to grow in Christ, we will need regular nurturing from the Scriptures: reading, studying, memorizing, and meditating on God's Word.[1] Next, new Christians will want to begin assimilating basic doctrines and truths about Jesus Christ's life, teachings, death, and resurrection. In time, we'll move on to learn more about the whole Bible and comprehend the more difficult concepts, the meat of the Word. Prayer will also become important in our lives. Thus a major healthy focus of Stage 2 growth is to *gain knowledge and understanding of God and his precepts.*

Community

In order to grow in Christ, fellowship with other Christians is essential. It is incongruent to think of a newborn being left alone after birth without someone to care for its needs of milk, clothing, protection, and so forth. An infant would not live many days in such circumstances. In some countries of the world, children several years old are forced to start fending for themselves. These "street children" eke out an existence among crime, glue-sniffing, and garbage—few reach anything we would call maturity. God's plan for the individual is the family; for the believer it is the church. So God has ordained Christian fellowship, an important ingredient in this stage of growth.

Doing

As the new infant grows, she starts following you with her eyes, reaches out, turns over, crawls, and later starts walking. Before you know it, this little girl is in college and has a family of her own. All of this is essential in the maturing process—and so it is with us spiritually.

Our spiritual lives need not only food, but exercise to grow and be healthy. As we learn to know what God wants through his Word and other Christians, the natural outcome will be doing what he tells us. In this second stage of growth, the focus is on "knowing" what God says and then "doing" it. We are to be "doers of the word, and not merely hearers" (James 1:22).

Most of Christendom is Strong on Stages 1 and 2

Stages 1 and 2—salvation; knowing and doing—are exceedingly important in our Christian lives. Thousands of books are written about the process of growth that corresponds to these stages. Fortunately, many of our churches and parachurch organizations are doing an outstanding job in promoting these areas of growth. Therefore, I am not devoting a lot of time and space to elaborate on these aspects of maturation. However, don't let the shortness of this chapter in any way minimize the crucial importance of Stage 2.

"My Burden Is Light"

Hopefully, in the process of being a Christ follower you will learn how to be fully dedicated to him without doing it out of compulsion, drivenness, or duty. You will discover that "His commandments are not burdensome" and that "[His] yoke is easy, and [His] burden is light" (1 John 5:3; Matthew 11:30). We can do this by keeping our focus on the person of Christ and emphasizing that our journey is first and foremost one of trust, love, and worship.

Christ wasn't driven. There is no evidence that he compulsively had a "quiet time" with the Father every morning, though we do know that he spent significant time in prayer and that he knew the Hebrew Scriptures very well. When his beloved friend

Lazarus was sick and died, Christ didn't rush to his side. When everyone was looking for him he felt no compulsion to meet all their needs. Rather, he specifically sought to follow what God instructed him to do. Somehow he maintained a wonderful, intimate relationship with the father, and he deeply cared about people. We need to discover how to follow in Christ's footsteps.

The Journey Ahead

As mentioned in chapter 1, it was in high school that Stage 2 growth became an important part of my life, and it was the epitome of my Christian life for the next several decades. Oh, I did take it to excess when working at the Servicemen's Center, but after my jolting experience in Oceanside and several months of rest, I learned to be a little kinder to my body. I joined the Navy and was trained in electronics, but the major thrust of my life was to share Christ with other sailors and disciple those who were willing to follow Jesus. They were basically good years, and I believe the Lord used me. However, the major emphasis of my life was *to know* God's Word and *to do* it. It would be years before I learned some of the deeper truths of the life of faith. Hopefully, it won't take you as long as it did me.

With Stages 1 and 2 an integral part of your life, you have gotten off to a good start on your journey. There are five additional stages that need to be considered if you are going to continue to mature in Christ. So let's move on "until Christ is fully developed in [our] lives" (Galatians 4:19 NLT).

The Pyramid of Spiritual Growth

As you can see, I have placed the second stage, the "To Know" and "To Do" stage, on top of the foundational stage of salvation in the Pyramid of Spiritual Growth (see *Illustration 4*). The "To

Know" and "To Do" are inserted on the same level with a dotted line between them because these two elements generally go together. Individuals generally pursue them at the same time, although one aspect may receive a greater emphasis than the other in any particular individual. Also you will note that I have made this tier larger as this stage in our lives rightfully receives a lot of attention as we learn to walk with God.

The Pyramid of Spiritual Growth

Illustration 4

Discussion Questions

1. Have you become a disciple of Christ—entering into the "To Know/To Do" Stage of spiritual living? Describe when it started, what the ingredients were, and how it is going now.

2. Do you think the focus of the first two stages of growth tends to be on oneself or God? Elaborate.

3. Children need black-and-white rules: never go into the street, don't touch the stove, and so forth. As the child matures, the rules aren't so clear cut. Describe whether there are, or are not, parallels in the spiritual world.

4. Do you think a Christian should have a daily, scheduled quiet time? Discuss the pros and cons.

5. Have you discovered how to be a true apprentice of Christ and still keep the burden "easy" and "light?" How do you do it?

6. If you have been a follower of Christ for years, has the character of your "knowing" and "doing" changed over time? How?

7. Mentors are often an important part of Stage 2. Who has been an important mentor or model for your life?

Experiencing God's Love and Grace This Week

Read and meditate on Galatians 4:19; Ephesians 4:13-14; I Corinthians 3:1-2; I Peter 2:1-3; Hebrews 5:12; Acts 17:11; Psalm 119:9-11; and I Timothy 4:15. Consider memorizing one or several of these verses. If you have time, read chapter 23, "How We Grow," in Rick Warren's *The Purpose-Driven Life* (Grand Rapids, MI: Zondervan, 2002).

10

The Authentic Heart

Stage 3: Being what you profess

I was 17 years old when I attended my first Navigator conference in the local mountains. Dawson Trotman, founder of The Navigators, needed some help unloading his car and I quickly volunteered. A dialog followed that resulted in my having an awful day. The time of my arising that morning came up and, without thinking, I quickly said that I had "gotten up at six o'clock to have my quiet time." The words had barely passed over my lips when my heart was smitten with the awareness that on that particular morning I had slept in. I don't think I heard a word that was said the entire day at the conference. I was in anguish over my lying to Daws to look good spiritually—and now, what to do about it! After a struggle, I finally was ready to confess it, not only to God, but also to Daws. To do this was complicated because Daws was not always easy to get to. Furthermore, many other people often surrounded him. This meant that I would probably have to confess my hypocrisy not only to him, but also to some other conferees. Finally, with a sigh of relief, I succeeded in confessing my transgression to him—and several others.

"Motives" Sliding Down the Slippery Slope

So what transpired in my original knee-jerk conversation? I was truly engaged in Stage 2 of spiritual growth, taking my walk with God seriously and endeavoring to know God's truths and to practice them. So far so good. I esteemed the leadership of the Navigators highly so I wanted to be viewed favorably by them. Herein is the crux of the problem. Whenever we are deeply involved in Stage 2 of spiritual growth, an "esprit de corps" develops with our fellow companions on our journey and with our mentors. We value them and want them to value us. But here is where it gets tricky—when our desire to be approved by people becomes more important than God's approval. This is exactly the slope the religious leaders of Christ's day found themselves sliding down (see John 5:44).

A similar phenomenon can also occur with productive activities that glorify God. For instance, God at one point instructed Moses to erect a bronze serpent so that the Israelites, who would otherwise die, could look on the serpent and be healed (Numbers 21:4-9). Later this bronze serpent became an idol and had to be destroyed (2 Kings 18:4).

In another example in Exodus and Numbers, we find God frequently numbering the Israelites. David counted his people in 2 Samuel 18 in accordance with God's command. Then when he counted the people in 2 Samuel 24, he met with God's disapproval and judgment. Why? A big factor seems to be David's motive. His commander had cautioned, "You have no right to rejoice in their strength" (2 Samuel 24:3 TLB). But David proceeded and afterward "was overwhelmed with guilt because he had counted the people, replacing trust with statistics" (2 Samuel 24:10 MSG).

In each situation, the heart's motives started out right but people, activities, or pride crept in and altruistic, godly things became sin. Christ's anger at the religious leaders of his day was over this very issue, which is why he said, "This people honors Me with their lips, but their heart is far away from Me" (Mark 7:6).

Satan has effectively deceived many of us Christians into believing that God's will and what he desires from us primarily involves what we do: how faithfully we read the Bible and have a quiet time, how often we witness, whether we tithe, serve on a committee, teach a class, feed the homeless, have a prison ministry, or carry out the 101 other activities of any active church. Don't get me wrong—these activities are very important. However, following God has more to do with our hearts than what we are doing for God. In fact, we can have our doctrine straight and even be martyrs for Christ, but if it hasn't transformed our lives from the inside out, it is literally worthless (1 Corinthians 13:1-3). *Ministry must flow out of our authentic being* or it is actually counterproductive.

The point is, that the most wonderful things in our Christian lives, things that can be supported right out of the Scriptures, if not done out of an genuine heart of trust and love of God, are not glorifying to God and, therefore, can actually be sin.

God Allows Weaknesses to Be Exposed

A genuine heart of trust and love is so important to God that he allows situations to arise that expose our areas of weakness. He says, "I, the LORD, search the heart, I test the mind, even to give to each man according to his ways" (Jeremiah 17:10). Solomon's weakness was women (1 Kings 11:4). Saul's lay in his desire for his people to think highly of him (1 Samuel 15:30). Eli's was his laissez faire attitude toward God's concerns (1 Samuel 2:22-36). Each of these men succumbed to his weakness and suffered as a result.

Becoming Aware

I have shared enough of my personal journey with you so you can see how some of these elements operated in my life. Sometimes a Christian activity—be it spiritual intake or service—can begin with the right motive but then change so that the good activities become problematic to our walk with Christ. In part, *I lost sight of God in my efforts for God and man.* My focus was on what I was doing for God rather than first and foremost trusting, loving, and worshiping God and allowing spiritual activities to flow from such a heart.

Throughout my spiritual pilgrimage, the Lord has periodically brought me up short about my heart attitude—the need for integrity in my heart before God. I introduced this chapter telling you about one such incident at age 17. However, as I look back on my life it was primarily during my 30s and early 40s when God particularly impressed this concept on my heart. I became aware that he was far less concerned about what I "knew" and "did" for him than the kind of person I was becoming on the inside. This was not really a new concept to me, but its meaning started to really sink in. "Knowing" and "Doing" were still important, mind you, but the crucial thing was that my life was being transformed into the image of God's Son. Now *"Being"* was imperative. God wanted authenticity in my life, and it had to start in my heart. If I am not the right kind of *person,* all my efforts are wood, hay, and stubble in God's eyes (1 Corinthians 3:11-15). This common quip sums it up: God made human *beings,* not human *doings.*

So I started placing a major emphasis on becoming the person I saw taught in the Scriptures. It's more than just "practicing what I was preaching." I was to first *"be* what I was preaching." The shift was subtle, and I doubt if someone observing my life perceived it. I continued to learn and do, but there was less focus on these activities and more emphasis on my heart attitude. People in this third stage of growth may do the same things as those in the second, but they do so with a *primary concern* that their hearts are authentic before God.

It's All About Heart

The crucial factor is *motive*. The crucial difference between Saul and David was not what they did or did not do—it was their heart attitudes. Saul tacitly acknowledged his sin but was more concerned about his appearance before the important people in his life. David's sin included taking a census, adultery, and murder—certainly the latter were worse by today's standards than Saul's sin. However, when David was confronted, he fully owned his sin and eventually went on to be described as a man after God's own heart. Saul skidded down the slope to infamy. Why the difference? David's motive ultimately centered around God, whereas Saul's motives were centered on himself.

There are times in Scripture when God overlooks the behavior because of the attitude of the person's heart. For example, Rahab the harlot lied, for which she is never criticized. In fact, she is listed in the lineage of Jesus and is commended for her faith (Matthew 1:5; Hebrews 11:31). When Peter lied by denying he knew Jesus, he received the Lord's disapproving look that caused him to "weep bitterly" (Luke 22:54-62). In both of these incidents, God's evaluation of the person wasn't based on the external act, but on the heart attitude. Rahab believed what she had heard about the awesomeness of the Israelite's God and acted to protect God's people (Joshua 2; 6:22-25). Peter, at this moment in his life, was acting selfishly to protect his own hide.

Rahab the prostitute had led a life full of lies and God apparently overlooked one more lie aimed to protect his people. He honored her newfound trust in him. She literally risked her life believing God would honor her faith. I am not advocating that the end justifies the means, but what I think is crucial is that *motive is everything.* God saw into her heart. He sees into the deepest crevices of our hearts. He knows our motives even when we don't (Psalm 139:23-24).

The motive of our heart is the most important facet of our lives. God told Samuel, "Do not look at his appearance…for God sees not as man sees, for man looks at the outward appearance, but the Lord looks at the heart" (1 Samuel 16:7). The Scriptures are filled with verses that address this crucial facet of our lives.[1]

Furthermore, true sanctification and spiritual transformation springs from the depths of our hearts. Out of it flows our will, choices, and actions. No wonder Christ said, "It's who you are, not what you say and do, that counts" (Luke 6:45 MSG).

Manifestations of the Authentic Heart

A heart that is genuinely centered on God will affect every area of a person's life. This is why the heart is so important. We are told, "For from [the heart] flow the springs of life" (Proverbs 4:23). Books are written on this subject, and we will discuss many facets of this in later chapters, but at this juncture I would like to highlight one important element.

Integrity with Messiness

One consequence of a heart and life that is right before God is that it will often appear messy. If we are going to walk before God with integrity of heart, certain aspects of our lives may appear to be messy to the world—especially the Christian world. I am defining messiness as apparent inconsistencies, doubts, and sometimes what appears to some as sin. However, as committed Christians we don't want messy lives, especially before our peer groups. If we are capable people living in Stage 2 and work hard to clean up the messiness on the outside, we may be able to do it—but then more will end up on the inside.

The facts are we all have a certain amount of messiness in our lives if we are honest. The biblical patriarch Abraham is a good example.[2] He started out well and had a series of personal encounters with the Almighty. He's remembered as a "friend of God" (James 2:23). But his life was punctuated with recurring lies and resorting to the flesh to accomplish God's purposes and protect himself. However, the true character of Abraham's heart is revealed when he was willing to sacrifice his son in faith and obedience.

David is another example of a person's life that was pretty messy. He vacillated between peaks of faith and valleys of sin. Again, when push came to shove, his life was characterized by honesty before God, faith, and adoration. Others could be added to this list such as Moses and Peter—but you get the idea. Messiness or inconsistency is the rule rather than the exception of the most esteemed God followers. Each of these men ultimately proved to have an authentic heart before God—and that is what counted.

Furthermore, you cannot follow God in your heart of hearts without violating some important *ideas* of Christians in your community. Thus your life will look messy even as Christ's did to the religious establishment of his day. God will see to it that there will be opportunities for you to follow Christ or please man— and you will *not* be able to do both. The only person who will *look* lily-white clean on both the inside and out will be the very capable individual stuck in Stage 2, who puts up a façade that makes the outside look nice and tidy while hiding the internal messiness.

The Heart of the Matter

Remember, *the most important attribute to God is the motive of our hearts* toward him. God wants us to have honest, pure, authentic hearts. This will cause us to *be* the kind of person he desires. This is the crux to causing our lives to be "changed from the inside out" (Romans 12:2 MSG). This is why we are told, "Keep your heart with all diligence, for out of it spring the issues of life" and "Above all else, guard your heart, for it affects everything you do" (Proverbs 4:23 NKJV and NLT).

The Pyramid of Spiritual Growth

We are now ready to add the third tier to our pyramid (see *Illustration 5*). This stage could be titled "The Pure Heart" or "The Changed Heart." A synonym to this would be "To Be" or "Being," referring to the fact that we should be on the inside what God desires and not just have it on the outside. However, I call this stage "The Authentic Heart," which captures all of these ideas.

The Pyramid of Spiritual Growth

Illustration 5

Discussion Questions

1. Was there a time in your life God impressed on you that he was much more concerned about the person you are rather than how much you knew and did for him? Describe.

2. Which do you think are most important: motives or actions? Why?

3. When your motives get messed up, how does it tend to manifest itself in your life?

4. Share a recent situation where you started out with good intentions, were walking in the Spirit, but slipped into the flesh or sin.

5. Think through and describe the messiness of someone's life from the Scriptures other than Abraham or David. What was God's response to him or her?

6. Do you agree with the author that a competent Stage 2 individual may look like he or she has his or her life more together than most individuals in Stage 3? Why?

7. What do you think of the statement "You cannot follow God in your heart without violating some important ideas of Christians in your community"?

Experiencing God's Love and Grace This Week

Read how Saul and David handled sin in their lives in 1 Samuel 15:1-35, and compare it with 2 Samuel 11:1–12:14; Psalm 51; and Acts 13:22. Consider their actions, heart attitudes, and results. How might you have responded in a situation similar to theirs?

You may want to read more about the importance of heart attitude in the Prelude and chapter 1 of Dallas Willard's *Renovation of the Heart* (Colorado Springs: NavPress, 2002).

Experiencing God

Stage 4: Developing an intimate relationship with God

It was the height of the Cuban missile crisis. The United States was one of the most powerful nations of the world, and John F. Kennedy, as president, was one of the most powerful men on the earth. An important meeting was taking place in the oval office. Security was tight. Guards protected the president with their lives. No one could get past them without the right credentials. Just then someone walked down the hall—the hall that only a select few could enter. He went past the guards and right into the oval office. No one challenged him; no one questioned who he was; no one asked him what business he had with the president. No one said the president was busy with a very important meeting. John-John, a two-year-old boy, walked into the oval office, interrupted the meeting, and jumped into the president's lap. The president put his arms around him and gave him his usual morning hug and kiss. Why was this boy accorded such privileges? It was because of a unique relationship—the president was his daddy.

In the same way we have a special relationship with God. He is waiting for us to jump into his lap, so to speak, and call him "Daddy." He wants us to have a personal, experiential relationship with him so that he can be fully involved in our lives. By faith we can enter into such a relationship.

What a contrast from living under the law! In the Old Testament the Israelites were struck dead if they even attempted to approach Mount Sinai to have an encounter with God. They were prohibited from entering the Holy of Holies in the tabernacle. In fact, they were afraid to say God's personal name, "Yahweh," because it was too sacred. When they read their Scripture, they would substitute the Hebrew word for "Lord."

But all this changed when God, through Christ, entered into our history in a personal way, making God accessible to everyone who desires to know him. Christ came in flesh and blood. He wants to have fellowship with us, typified by the most down-to-earth symbol: to dine with us. In the Middle East, sharing a meal means that an ongoing relationship has been established by the one offering hospitality—your lives are now connected. Jesus came, not speaking a foreign or erudite language. He communicated in the common language of the day. He was, and is, Emmanuel—God with us! God was with us when he walked the earth for 33 years embodied in the person of Jesus Christ. No wonder the Scriptures say we have a "personal God" (Romans 15:5 MSG). Today we can experience his presence so much more than when Christ physically walked with his apprentices because we have the Holy Spirit, the Paraclete, who has come to reside *in* us and commune with us as an integral part of our daily lives.

Invitation to an Intimate Experience

We Have a Personal, Immanent God

God is available and waiting for us to jump into his lap. We can have a personal, experiential relationship with God. He is immanent—that is, his presence is fully involved in our lives.

The Scriptures record that God walked with Adam and Eve. God was present when Cain killed Abel. He walked with Enoch; he entered into a discussion with Noah. And this accounts for only the first six chapters of the Bible! All this leads me to the point that God's involvement with human beings can be seen throughout history—virtually on every page of Holy Writ. If we deny his immanence, we rob God and ourselves of his personal involvement and presence in our lives. This would be a giant loss. God has not left planet Earth; he is closer than a brother, sister, or spouse.

We Affect God's Feelings

When the prodigal son left home, I don't think the father wore a smile on his face. Instead he had a look of loving concern. He probably even felt deep grief and disappointment at his son's departure. He hurt because he loved his son so much. When the prodigal came to his senses and returned home, the story shows the father's elation: running to greet him (unheard of in his culture), falling on his neck, kissing him, putting a robe over his shoulders, placing a ring on his finger, and giving him a party. The father was delighted to see his boy. (See Luke 15.)

But the prodigal had to come to his senses and *choose* to return home in order to experience his father's embrace and love. Only then did his father's love become apparent. Yes, this is a parable, but it's a parable from Jesus about our heavenly Father's response to a child returning to his father. This accurately depicts the Father's relationship to us, his children. He has a deep, parental love and longing for all of us not only to return to him, but also to have an interactive, emotional relationship with him. He wants us to come out from the lonely, sweaty fields and enjoy his party.

We, as his children, affect the Triune God. Here again Christ demonstrated God's feelings for us when he was so moved by those around him. He wept with Mary over Lazarus' death (John 11:35), he was angry with the religious leaders of the day because of their hard, calloused hearts (Mark 3:5), and we find him agonizing in the garden (Matthew 26:38). These are just a few of the emotions Jesus had as a direct result of people around him. Similarly, we can see that God can be grieved (Genesis 6:6-7; Psalm 78:40; Ephesians 4:30). God took pleasure in David (1 Chronicles 28:4), but when he did evil God was clearly upset with him (2 Samuel 11:27–12:13). God loved the baby Solomon and was pleased with Solomon's good choices (2 Samuel 12:24-25; 1 Kings 3:10), but later, due to bad choices, God was angry with him (1 Kings 11:9). These are only a brief sampling of passages that express the variety of God's feelings. It is clear that we have a Father who is deeply touched by our lives (Hebrews 4:15 KJV).

A.W. Tozer says, "God is a Person, and in the deep of His mighty nature He thinks, wills, enjoys, feels, loves, desires and suffers as any other person may."[1] Similarly, Curtis and Eldredge, in *The Sacred Romance*, state, "We affect [God]. We impact the members of the Trinity as truly as they do each other."[2] Pastor Rick Warren writes, "We often forget that God has emotions, too. He feels things very deeply. The Bible tells us that God grieves, gets jealous and angry, and feels compassion, pity, sorrow, and sympathy as well as happiness, gladness, and satisfaction. God loves, delights, gets pleasure, rejoices, enjoys, and even laughs!"[3] Tim Dearborn, in *Taste & See*, says, "We worship and serve a God of passion....God himself is disturbed by the pain of his creation and rejoices over its beauty and goodness."[4] The fact that God is affected by people's actions, choices, and emotions in no way alters his basic character or nature, which will never change.

God Should Affect Our Feelings

Our relationship with God not only affects God's feelings but should affect our feelings as well. As long as our feelings don't control us but are an outgrowth of a life with Christ, they are a wonderful aspect of our personalities. After all, God gave us our feelings to enjoy and experience. J.I. Packer says, "We must not lose sight of the fact that knowing God is an emotional relationship, as well as an intellectual and volitional one, and could not indeed be a deep relation between persons were it not so. The believer is, and must be, emotionally involved."[5]

In fact, we long for a deep, experiential relationship with our God whether we are aware of it or not. Ken Gire, in *Windows of the Soul: Experiencing God in New Ways*, says, "We long for something more than a routine walk around the religious block. We long for the companionship of God. We long for the assurance that we are not taking this journey alone. That He is walking with us and talking with us and intimately involved in our lives."[6]

It Takes Two to Have a Relationship

Klaus Issler, in *Wasting Time with God: A Christian Spirituality of Friendship with God*, says, "The Bible teaches that a continuing relationship with God requires the participation of both parties: 'Come near to God and he will come near to you' (James 4:8). Our love relationship with God can *always* grow deeper and deeper."[7] Like the prodigal son, we can run from our heavenly Father, and it will cause him sorrow. Or we can return to the Father, accept his embrace, and have an intimate relationship with him. God wants us to enjoy his presence—but the choice is ours.

As A.W. Tozer says, *"God wills that we should push on into His Presence and live our whole life there. This is to be known to us in conscious experience.... every moment of every day.... The world is* perishing for lack of the knowledge of God and the Church is famishing for want of His Presence. The instant cure of most of our religious ills would be to enter the Presence in *spiritual experience.*"[8]

God Can and Wants to Be Known

God is near and wants to be known. We see this initially when God walked and talked with Adam and Eve. When sin caused them to hide from God, he still went looking for them, calling "Adam, where are you?" Unfortunately, sin has continued to interfere with our relationship with God, but his desire for fellowship remains unchanged. He, as in the garden, is calling out and looking for people who desire to know and experience him in a real and authentic manner—these are the people in whom God delights.

Obstacles to Our Relationship with God

If God desires a living, emotional, interactive relationship with us and it is so beneficial to us—what keeps us from pursuing it? Let me highlight a few obstacles.

Childhood Relationships Affect
Our Relationship with God

For all of us the nature of our early relationships affect how we view our heavenly Father. My father was the son of a sharecropper who could barely eke out a living for his family of 14 children. My father used to tell about their mealtimes in Sweden: The family would sit around the table and the food was served from the oldest to the youngest. Since my dad was the twelfth child, sometimes there was no food left on the serving plate by the time it reached him. This poverty left its scars on the family. For example, his older sister used to tell how upset she was when yet another child was born. Among 12 boys there were only 2 girls, and they bore a large part of the parenting role. Once she was so frustrated over the birth of yet another child for whom she would have to care that she rocked the cradle so hard that the baby (my dad) flew right out of it!

As Grandfather was able to save money, he sent his children, a few at a time, to America—the land of opportunity. My dad, after immigrating to the United States at nine years of age and with only a fifth-grade education, determined that he would be a faithful provider for his family and be loyal to God—a goal he was able to accomplish. However, I never remember sitting on his lap, playing ball with him, or being praised for anything. Dad was emotionally absent, undoubtedly stemming from what he experienced in his childhood. With his Scandinavian stoicism and the pop psychology of the day—"don't praise children as it will go to their heads"—and probably his own lack of emotional nurturing, I never experienced an interactive, loving relationship with my father. I never heard him say "well done" or that he loved me...until very late in his life—and then only after I told him I loved him. For the most part we had an emotionless relationship. Oh, I intellectually knew he loved me, but I didn't feel it. It was almost as though his face was frozen.

Unfortunately that reality has had an adverse effect on me, not only in general, but particularly in my relationship with my heavenly Father. Not sensing my father's love, I worked hard to gain it, and the same feeling carried over to my Christian life. For many decades my relationship with my heavenly Father was essentially emotionless. Often I *felt* I was walking the journey alone. Sure, I believed in God. I knew intellectually he was there and loved me, but experientially I didn't feel his love and presence.

I had little sense of an interactive, mutually responsive relationship with him.

A Misunderstanding About What "Knowing" Means

Another giant obstacle to our relationship with God is a misunderstanding about what it means to "know God." A lot of people talk about knowing God. Early in my Christian life I memorized Philippians 3:10, which emphasizes "that I may know him." Again, I am grateful to the Navigators for their positive influence on my life. Their motto includes "To Know Him." But with all the emphasis on Bible study and memorizing the Word, the message I took home was "that I may know the Bible." Knowing the Bible, knowing intellectually about God, knowing doctrine—all of this is important, but such knowledge is not the same as knowing Christ the way a husband knows his wife or a wife her husband. In fact, throughout Scripture "knowing" conveys this deep involvement with another. God wants to have this kind of intimate relationship with us. Head knowledge is so different from heart experience. Eugene Peterson says the psalms "are not provided to teach us about God but to train us in responding to him."[9] Cognitive information is completely different than experiential appreciation. It can be as dissimilar as knowing what food is to actually eating food. In fact, this is exactly the issue over which the Pharisees and many of Christ's own disciples stumbled. Christ referred to himself as the "living bread of life," the one they had to "eat," to know intimately, so that he might become a part of them. Knowing about Christ and living in an intimate relationship with Christ are as different as night and day. Klaus Issler says, "Unfortunately, within the traditional categories of theology, the subject of a relationship with God is unintentionally deemphasized, although it should be preeminent above any other aspect of Christian living….Scripture always makes our relationship with God the ultimate focus and goal of Christian living."[10]

A Deep, Intimate Experience

Up to this point in my life, God so often seemed distant and our relationship emotionless. But in my 40s and 50s it started to dawn on me that he wanted an interactive, emotional relationship with me. These truths propelled me into this phase of growth— Stage 4. It made me aware that in addition to having an authentic heart before God, God desired that I experience a *personal relationship with him.* Here are some of the principles that I found helpful.

Fostering an Experiential Relationship with God

Practicing the Presence of God

The classic little book *The Practice of the Presence of God* by Brother Lawrence was a significant catalyst in helping me in my relationship with God. Brother Lawrence was a monk in the seventeenth century who wanted to devote his life to God but was placed in the monastery kitchen. Nevertheless, he worked constantly at being aware of God's presence. "His one desire was for communion with God." He encourages us "that we should establish ourselves in a sense of God's presence by continually conversing with Him…in order to form a habit of conversing with God continually, and referring all we do to Him, we must first apply to Him with some diligence." When his thoughts would wander he concluded "that useless thoughts spoil all…that we ought to reject them as soon as we perceived their impertinence to the matter in hand…and return to our communion with God." Though this practice requires diligence, it is not hard: "We need only to recognize God intimately present with us."[11] So learning to focus our attention on God assists in our experiencing a relationship with him.

Look for the Lord

We also need to look for the Lord. We need to see and experience him in the Scriptures and to look for his presence and activity in all of life. Once when the biblical patriarch Jacob was in a crisis while traveling in the open countryside, he had an encounter with God through a dream. When he awoke he said: "Surely the LORD is in this place, and I did not know it....How awesome is this place! This is none other than the house of God, and this is the gate of heaven" (Genesis 28:16-17). What had been a dream in the wide open spaces of the Middle East was recognized as the gate of heaven. Jacob became aware of the Lord's presence in the situation. But it didn't stop there. Jacob had several more crises of faith, and again he went back to the same location, built an altar to God, and this time discovered that God himself was there (Genesis 35:1-15).

There was a time when the Syrian army surrounded Elisha and his servant. The servant didn't see God's hand in the situation as his master did, so understandably he was frightened. But Elisha said, " 'Do not fear, for those who are with us are more than those who are with them.' Then Elisha prayed and said, 'O LORD, I pray, open his eyes that he may see.' And the LORD opened the servant's eyes and he saw; and behold, the mountain was full of horses and chariots of fire all around [protecting] Elisha" (2 Kings 6:16-18). So with the help of the Holy Spirit we can start to see the Lord and his workings all around us.

We need to learn to be sensitive to God's presence in our everyday environment. God and his activities surround us like the air. He is continually involved in the world, and too often we aren't even aware of it. He is at work in the routine things that we do: driving to work, doing the dishes, talking to people, and even in the obstacles that complicate our daily lives. As our eyes are opened to the fact that God is at work in our lives, we will experience a new sense of his presence.

Avoid the Rat Race

People talk about taking time to smell the roses. To practice the presence of the Lord, to be led by his Spirit moment by moment takes time. Tozer says, "In coming to God we should place ourselves in His presence with the confidence that He is the aggressor, not we. He has been waiting to manifest Himself to us till such time as our noise and activity have subsided enough for Him to make Himself heard and felt by us."[12] Some speak about our need for "margin"—that is, unscheduled time in our lives.[13] If every minute is so tightly scheduled, it's almost impossible to hear the still, small voice of God and be sensitive to his leading. One needs unscheduled time to listen to God. Tim Dearborn says:

> If we want to learn to see the presence of God, we need to walk slowly. Spiritual directors call this the spiritual act of "noticing." Most of us don't notice our spiritual surroundings. We're so busy watching what we're leaving (our failures, guilt and triumphs) or what we're trying to get to (our hopes, fears and dreams) that we don't notice where we are now. As a result, we miss seeing the signs of the presence of God all around us.[14]

What Is Your God Like?

Does God walk with you on your journey? Is the face of your God frozen like the images on Mount Rushmore? As you read this book I pray that you will see your heavenly Father as loving you, wooing you, and wanting you to have an intimate, *interactive* relationship with him. May you see the *responsive* face of Jesus!

The Pyramid of Spiritual Growth

Illustration 6 shows the pyramid with the addition of the fourth stage of growth: An Experiential Relationship.

The Pyramid of Spiritual Growth

Illustration 6

Discussion Questions

1. Do you *feel* a personal, experiential relationship with Christ? Is there any other type of relationship?

2. What has been your conscious experience with God this last week?

3. To what extent do you think living in his presence will solve most of our religious and interpersonal ills?

4. Have you endeavored to practice the presence of God? How has that worked out for you?

5. How have the important people in your early years affected your image of God?

6. Some Christians don't believe we affect God's emotions. What do you think? What might be the consequences of believing God is or is not affected by our actions, choices, and emotions?

7. What is your God like? What do you see when you look into his face?

Experiencing God's Love and Grace This Week

During this week practice the presence of God. Whenever you have free moments, focus on God. Be reminded of his love for you. Thank him for who he is and that you have a relationship with him. Shoot up a brief prayer for the situation at hand. Be open to God in your world through the avenue of your feelings and emotions. If you have never read the short but classic paperback by Brother Lawrence, *The Practice of the Presence of God* (Old Tappan, NJ: Spire Books, 1969), I strongly recommend it to you.

12

The Crises of Faith

Stage 5: Successfully navigating
life's difficulties

My brother, Dr. Paul Carlson, was a medical missionary in the Congo. He began his work in a jungle village less than a year before the 1964 Simba uprising. At 36 years of age, he was taken captive at his hospital and rebel soldiers shot members of his staff before his eyes. During the three months he was held prisoner, he was beaten and falsely accused of being a mercenary and a spy. Paul certainly had a crisis of faith.

My own crisis of faith, although not nearly as dramatic as Paul's, came when I was an intern working 90 hours a week. During this time, Paul's status was being reported constantly in the news media. Reporters called me frequently. In the middle of all this, my mother had a severe heart attack. Together we agonized over Paul's situation as a hostage. We prayed for his release, but finally, in our own desperation and feeling for the suffering Paul was going through, we asked God that whatever the final result, might it come quickly. Within a week he was martyred. What a difficult time for us all. Questions came from around the world, asking why God would allow such a catastrophe. This crisis of faith occurred when I was 31 years old.

Crises of faith can occur at any age, and they come in various forms. My second significant crisis came when I was 47. A patient of mine committed suicide. The fact that we had many mutual friends at church made this even more difficult. My seeming failure to help him threatened my sense of competence as a psychiatrist and physician. Though the average psychiatrist loses a patient to suicide every eight years, this one threw me for a loop. I went into a major depression despite my adamantly seeking God by spending much time in prayer and the Word. Regardless of all my efforts to seek him, God seemed so remote. It also didn't help when a pastor wrote to me to tell me I was in sin. It was truly a "dark night of the soul" although a better description for me would have been a "dark year of the soul."[1]

When I was 52, my only daughter was diagnosed with acute leukemia. For two years she teetered between life and death, spending eight months in the hospital. The cancer recurred, and we were told there was no hope of her living. I cried and pleaded with God, almost shaking my fist at him—but ultimately yielded her life to him. The upshot of a long story, which is told in *When Life Isn't Fair,* is that she is alive and well 20 years later![2]

A different kind of crisis came when I was 57. I verbalized a doctrinal position that did not exactly conform to views of some Christians with whom I frequently associate. Furthermore, as a psychiatrist I have taken a position that not all emotional illness is the result of the personal sin of the sufferer. As a result, key individuals criticized me and some have effectively censored me. As strange as it might seem, the pain associated with feeling judged by believers with whom I frequently come into contact is as hard to handle as some of the earlier crises of faith in my life.

Not *If,* But *When*

Crises affect everyone. Some are rather trivial: a dented fender, the loss of a sale, or a "D" on a term paper. Others are monumental:

premature death of a loved one, a hurricane destroying your home, or the loss of your pension fund when you are 65 and have no other resources. And of course, there is everything in between. Some crises impact people differently. The death of a cat may be trivial to one person, but to a five-year-old or someone without other close companionship, it may be monumental. Likewise, some crises impact our faith in God and others do not. I am defining a "crisis of faith" as any adverse event in our lives that in some way impacts our belief or relationship with God.

We may be confronted by a crisis of faith at any time in our walk with God. Some individuals come to faith through a crisis; others will face obstacles and tragedies later in their spiritual journey. But one thing is certain. There will be at least one or more crises of faith in your lifetime.

Gospel writer Mark tells us, "Everyone's going through a refining fire sooner or later" (Mark 9:49 MSG). Paul says, "Indeed, all who desire to live godly in Christ Jesus will be persecuted" (2 Timothy 3:12). Peter cautions, "Dear friends, don't be bewildered or surprised when you go through the fiery trials ahead, for this is no strange, unusual thing that is going to happen to you. Instead, be really glad—because these trials will make you partners with Christ in his suffering, and afterwards you will have the wonderful joy of sharing his glory" (1 Peter 4:12-13 TLB). Paul reminds the Philippians, "There's far more to this life than trusting in Christ. There's also suffering for him. And the suffering is as much a gift as the trusting" (Philippians 1:29 MSG).

We need to see crises as normal for followers of Christ. "God is educating you; that's why you must never drop out. He's treating you as dear children. This trouble you're in isn't punishment; it's training" (Hebrews 12:7 MSG). Often we have to be brought to the end of ourselves before we can grow into Christian maturity.

In fact, sometimes we have to hit bottom before we can progress. God wants us to realize that we can't overcome sin by strengthening our own flesh. Only in our weakness and crucified flesh does God work. The degree to which the flesh is broken and yielded to God is the degree to which he can bless us. Billy Graham says, "The key to experiencing supernatural, liberating strength is *personal weakness*. That's right, personal weakness. God's power 'shows up best in weak people' (2 Corinthians 12:9 TLB)....The weaker you are, the more God's strength can 'show up' in you."[3]

Ed is a wonderful friend. He's a dedicated Christian, personable, capable, and a highly respected space scientist. He yielded his life to God in college and became intent on doing things right, living for God, and exercising Christian leadership. He took these qualities into his marriage. He was very articulate, able to get his way, and be in control—that is, until ten years into his marriage when his wife refused to allow that kind of domination to continue. He was willing to lay down his life for his wife and couldn't comprehend why his marriage and life were in such a tailspin. He describes seven years of torment as he plummeted into depression. Ed, a very social individual, tells how lonely he felt during this time. One night he drove to a friend's house and from his car window he could see his friend socializing with other friends, all of whom he knew. But Ed felt like an outsider and drove away. It was the loneliest time in his life. People didn't know what to say, and he sensed it. He was involved in a nonacceptable crisis—a messy marital conflict.

My wife and I were in a small group with Ed and his wife, Millie, at the time. Ed and I occasionally saw each other, and we even had breakfast together—but I certainly wasn't the friend I might have been. I was busy raising a young family, starting a medical practice, and had to hurry up to church to tend to my duties as church chairman and teach Bible classes. I was too busy about God's work to be a Good Samaritan.

You see, we Christians have acceptable and nonacceptable crises. An acceptable crisis is a heart attack, cancer, or a flooded house. But there are many nonacceptable crises: mental illness, marital discord, alcoholism, and God forbid that you or your child should have homosexual tendencies, to name a few. The nonacceptable crises have a double whammy—the original problem, plus the nonacceptance by many in the Christian community. It is clear how Christ feels about all of this—he went out of his way to befriend the unacceptable of his day—the adulterer, prostitute, and shady tax collector.

Getting back to Ed, it was only when the divorce papers were presented to him that he finally relinquished control and began to rebuild his marriage. It is now 30 years later, and he says this experience positively revolutionized his life. He learned gratitude, forgiveness, grace, and how to better follow Jesus. He now is a wonderful example of the life of faith, which we will be discussing in the next chapter. He is positively influencing scores of lives for the kingdom of God.

Every patriarch in the Old Testament whom God used went through his own crisis of faith that required the relinquishment of control over his life. Abraham had to travel to an unknown land and be willing to literally kill his son, Isaac. Moses had to return to the land where he was wanted for murder and lead a rebellious people out of Egypt (to name only a few of his many crises). The New Testament saints likewise went through their difficult times. Paul faced a multitude of difficulties: a troubling physical weakness, persecution, shipwreck, imprisonment, beatings, and ultimately martyrdom. In fact, according to tradition, 11 of the 12 disciples were martyrs for their faith.

As we read the accounts of saints since biblical times, they universally went through their crises of faith. Dr. Raymond Edman describes the lives of 20 eminent Christians, and they all went through "trials, heartaches, searching and groping." A brief survey reveals that the great preacher Charles Finney found himself "verging fast to despair." The famous evangelist Dwight L. Moody describes a deep dissatisfaction of his heart. Even the great pioneer missionary to China Hudson Taylor, who experienced the exhilarating "Exchanged life" which we will discuss in detail in the next chapter, struggled with "days of sorrow and nights of heaviness….through a physical breakdown…[he had] a badly deranged liver [that] made him sleepless and led to painful depression of spirit."[4]

I can't think of one saint whom God used who didn't go through his or her crisis. They often referred to it as the "dark night of the soul"—a time when God seemed very distant or absent from their lives. Some of their lives ended in martyrdom. In fact, *Fox's Book of Martyrs* is an account of the persecution and often martyrdom of countless saints from the time of apostles through the 1800s. My brother gave my copy to me, little knowing that he himself would be murdered for his faith. During the early rumblings of trouble and just a few months before Paul was taken prisoner, he reminded the Congolese church that more people had been martyrs in that generation than in all previous generations. This statement remains true today: There are more martyrs during our generation than in all past generations put together. This reality is a far cry from the consumer-oriented Christianity so often promoted both in and outside the church today.

What Happened to the "Wonderful Life"?

Most of us have been exposed to the teaching that "God has a wonderful plan for your life." Does the concept that we should expect crises negate this teaching? No, it doesn't. But we must understand what God's having a "wonderful plan" does and does not mean. Certainly in the overall view of eternity, God does have a wonderful plan for our lives. However, in this life God allows both good and evil. Frankly, sometimes God's plans do not *appear* good for many people on this earth. Yet for most of us in the free world, the life he gives us is pretty good. But we must learn to expect the right things from God and to view life from an eternal perspective.

If It's Not One Crisis, It's Another

Crises of faith take innumerable forms. Sometimes they arise as a direct result of our own negligence or outright sin. But just as often they result from the sin-sick world in which we live. They can come through the weakness of our fallen bodies in the form of medical illnesses or suffering. The primary target can be our emotions or minds. It may be business reverses, a wayward child, or criticism from others. Chronic "little crises" can quickly add up and become as monumental as the "big crises." These can be stresses in the home or workplace, conflicts with others, financial pressures, failed aspirations, or even a sense that we have let someone else down. These all have great potential for affecting our walk of faith.

Sometimes other Christians cause crises. Probably the most difficult to deal with is the child or young person who has been abused by a religious leader. It could be sexually, but often it is a harsh, graceless Christianity. Often these individuals spend the rest of their lives trying to put the pieces of their lives back together but never succeed. Many won't darken the door of a church again, but others, still wounded, sit in pews each Sunday.

The sensitive Christian often finds that misunderstanding and criticism are inevitable, often coming from Christians, which make these the hardest crises to deal with. This is especially true when one strives to tell the truth and live with honesty, openness, and authenticity within the Christian community. The book *TrueFaced* refers to "the reality of suffering. Not the suffering from sickness, accidents, or unfortunate circumstances, but the suffering that comes from aligning ourselves with truth, with truth telling."[5] Many religious communities won't accept total truthfulness if it goes against their mores. If someone crosses the line, censorship is likely. Thus there is a risk in telling the truth—and often it can be costly. So the tendency for most Christians is to put on a mask. But if we are going to reach new heights in our spiritual journeys, the masks must be pulled off. Some wounds are inevitable.

It can be very expensive personally to be totally honest and yield our wills to God. Marguerite Porete, a thirteenth-century saint, wrote on experiencing the love of God and stages of growth. She felt yielding her will to God was so important that she devoted two of her seven stages to that pursuit. "Christians" burned her at the stake for what she believed.[6]

The Crisis of Reevaluation of Faith

Sometimes the biggest crisis of faith can be *a reevaluation of one's faith*. In order to grow, every believer must reevaluate what he or she has been taught and must discover in prayer and God's Word what to continue to embrace and what to discard in order to keep growing.

As I look back on my life there were several decades when I thought I had things pretty well figured out in the Christian life. No doubt there was some pride in my understanding of spiritual issues, and I had a personal satisfaction that I had no need to modify my beliefs. In recent years I can see how wrong I was. The modifications for me are not in the underlying core beliefs, but in shades of understanding the Christian life.

Throughout Scripture this reevaluation is often a necessary step in journeys of faith. For instance, it occurs in Peter's arguing with a voice from heaven telling him to eat forbidden food (Acts 10:9-29) and in Paul's Damascus experience (Acts 9:1-19). Scott Peck has only four stages of spiritual growth in his model, but one of those stages focuses on this very issue. He believes it is a necessary step and calls it the "Skeptic" or "Individual" stage.[7] This can leave one standing alone with God, which can feel scary and far away from the comfortable, approving environment of Stage 2—knowing God's truths and doing them. However, such a move is a necessary prerequisite if one is going to grow to maturity "until Christ is formed in [us]" (Galatians 4:19).

Janet Hagberg and Robert Guelich in *The Critical Journey: Stages in the Life of Faith* talk about "the Wall." They describe it as a confrontation with God and our own will. It is a willingness to question what we think to be true and to allow God to enlighten us. It means owning and dealing with our doubts. They go on to make a shocking statement for us to consider:

> It would be great to think that most…spiritual leaders could be our guides through…[this stage] and the Wall. The sad truth is that many of these leaders have not been led through this stage themselves and have not allowed themselves to question deeply or to become whole. So many of those to whom we often look most naturally for help are inadequate

guides for this part of the journey. Those who have been
through this stage themselves…are unique people and are
to be sought out.[8]

Stop! Understand the Problem

In order to find an appropriate solution to any difficulty or
crisis, we first need a proper diagnosis. Only when we determine
the specific cause of a problem can we take the right steps to
resolve the issue. If the problem is sin, we need to be ruthlessly
honest about that. We must confess it, forsake it, and yield to any
appropriate discipline. Often we can find others to blame, and
many times they share some responsibility—but we must boldly
own all the culpability that is ours.

On the other hand, adversity and crises of faith are among the
most difficult struggles Christians face. There can be a great tendency for many individuals to assume they are responsible for
them. But before we accept in a knee-jerk fashion that we are
automatically responsible for our current crisis, we need to
examine the possible causes before the Lord. If we have honestly
searched our hearts before God and there is no unforgiven past
sin or current state of disobedience, we should not assume that we
are responsible for the unfortunate situation. There are many
causes for crises, and we don't do God or ourselves a good service
if we accept responsibility when we are not responsible.

Now, What About Our Response?

I am convinced that *how* we respond to crises is more important than *what* the crisis is or what caused the crisis in the first
place—*even if it is due to our own sin.*

Repentance

Repentance, remorse, and a contrite heart are the hallmarks of a saint (though fallen). The one who bristles, defends, excuses, and compensates through "the flesh" is no saint at all. When Samuel confronted Saul about his disobedience to God's commands regarding the destruction of Amalek, he replied, "I did obey the voice of the LORD, and went on the mission on which the LORD sent me....*But* the people took some of the spoil...to sacrifice to the LORD your God at Gilgal" (1 Samuel 15:20-21). In contrast, when Nathan prophesied judgment on David for his sin of murdering Uriah, there were no ifs, ands, or buts. David responded, "*I have sinned* against the LORD" (2 Samuel 12:13). Psalms 32 and 51 portray for us further the depth and sincerity of his repentance, as well as the blessing and healing of God's complete forgiveness.

Surrender

When crises confront us and we have taken appropriate steps in dealing with them, sometimes the difficulties still do not turn out the way we would like. We then are confronted with a choice of yielding to God's will in the matter. We can surrender or resist. If we want to see God redeem what seems like a bad situation, we need to surrender to God's will. This involves not only what we say and do, but more importantly, *the attitude of our hearts*. The Scriptures contain numerous examples of both resisting and surrendering: The rich young ruler was not willing to surrender his riches; King Saul was not willing to surrender his reputation; Jonah resisted God's ultimate intent for Nineveh. In contrast: Abraham was willing to surrender his son Isaac; Jeremiah surrendered his ideas of a prophet's ministry; and Paul accepted

God's answer of "no" when he asked that his "thorn in the flesh" be removed. Only with surrender will God redeem a situation.

For some of you who read this, it will immediately remind you of some past point in your lives when you refused to follow God's will: You had an abortion, married the wrong person, were unwilling to go to the mission field, or whatever. The past is just that, it is past. At this point in time, God's primary concern is that you are *now* surrendered to him. Satan would love to pin the past situation on you and have you think that you are destined to be a second-class Christian. Remember, God's compassions are new every morning (Lamentations 3:22-23). When the prodigal returned he wasn't received grudgingly and treated harshly. God is the God of second (and third and fourth...) chances (see Jonah 3:1). God loves you! What is crucial is that at this moment in time you are totally surrendered to him and his will for your life.

In fact, some who read this may have made some hard choices in the past for God: You went to the mission field and made other great sacrifices, but now you are resentful about your financial situation, angry with the field director, or some other troubling issue. This state of mind is compromising your life and any further growth in Christ. The issue is always this: Surrender—*today*— *now*.

God Meant It for Good

Joseph went through a series of crises over a number of years. Though he contributed to the alienation of his brothers by calling attention to his favored position with his father, his brothers truly were scoundrels. But clearly God uses Joseph's ill treatment for good (Genesis 50:20). Joseph provides just one illustration of this universal truth: "And we know that God causes all things to work together for good to those who love God, to those who are called according to His purpose" (Romans 8:28). This verse remains true no matter who is to blame for the current problem. But for God to bring good out of a bad situation, we must yield the issue and ourselves to him. If we refuse, we become a "Resistant Christian" and all bets are off.

Benefit of Crises

The individual who goes through a crisis will emerge a different person. You cannot go through a difficulty without either regressing or growing—and the greater the crisis, the greater the potential loss or gain. A crisis never leaves us the same—and hopefully our choices will make it a gain for the kingdom and for us. Crises typically spur us on to the next stage of growth.

A crisis of faith is an opportunity of faith. We have the opportunity to become kind, tender, compassionate people with greater understanding, able to lead and to comfort others (2 Corinthians 1:3-10). In fact:

> You're blessed when you're at the end of your rope. With less of you there is more of God and his rule. You're blessed when you feel you've lost what is most dear to you. Only then can you be embraced by the One most dear to you (Matthew 5:3-4 MSG).

> And now, isn't it wonderful all the ways in which this distress has goaded you closer to God? You're more alive, more concerned, more sensitive, more reverent, more human, more passionate, more responsible. Looked at from any angle, you've come out of this with purity of heart. And that is what I was hoping for in the first place (2 Corinthians 7:11-12 MSG).

It is no wonder Paul reminds us that "we also rejoice in our sufferings, because we know that suffering produces perseverance; perseverance, character; and character, hope. And hope does not disappoint us, because God has poured out his love into our hearts by the Holy Spirit, whom he has given us" (Romans 5:3-5 NIV).

It makes good sense that the two Chinese characters that make up the English word "crisis" are "danger" and "opportunity." When confronted with a crisis, we face the dangerous situation of choosing the path of the flesh and our lives going down the road to infamy. Or we can surrender our lives to God and reap the opportunity of a lifetime. God gives us that choice.

I'm reminded of renowned pastor Gordon MacDonald. He refers to some personal crises of faith in his life by using the boxing analogy of "knockouts." He describes five such "knockouts," and says they were "all my responsibility." But he goes on to say they were "important markers in my life of following Jesus." The most difficult one was when he "failed [his] wife and...marriage." He says, "I began to live with a secret....I told myself that death would be preferable." Nevertheless, "We came to know a combination of sadness and grace that will never be put into words." As he faced his sin, a godly man told him that one day he would look back and say: "Those were some of the most important days of my life." Gordon MacDonald responded: "Speaking of knockouts! I would have liked to [have] knocked him out for saying such a thing. But years later, I learned he was right...I came to a deeper, more accurate, more humbling awareness of my deeper self than I would have ever reached under other circumstances. I learned about the magnificence of God's kindness."[9]

God Only Uses Cracked Pots that Limp

Paul refers to our weakness and failures, and says we're ordinary clay pots, or, if you will, "cracked pots." God uses such pots only in their weakness, so that praise and glory can go to him and not us (2 Corinthians 4:7-17; 12:7-10).

I have heard it said, "I want to follow someone who is limping," alluding to the story of Jacob's wrestling with God (Genesis 32:24-32). This statement means that such a person wants to follow the guidance and footsteps of someone who had his or her struggles but worked through them and left with the touch of God—a limp. After all is said and done, God only uses cracked pots that limp.

The Pyramid of Spiritual Growth

In *Illustration 7* there's now a fifth tier to the Pyramid of Spiritual Growth. Although various crises occur at several points in our lives, for the sake of simplicity and illustration, I have noted it at this point in the pyramid.

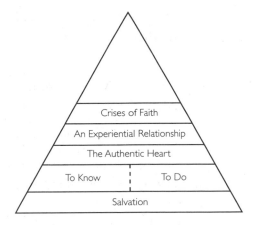

The Pyramid of Spiritual Growth

Illustration 7

Your personal pyramid of spiritual growth will undoubtedly look different from this one. Possibly you haven't had a crisis of faith yet. Some will have had a single crisis, yet others may have experienced a series of crises. I believe that the successful navigation of a crisis is probably a prerequisite for fully entering the next two magnificent stages to spiritual maturity.

Discussion Questions

1. How did you do this last week at practicing the presence of God? Share your experience with others.

2. Do you think crises are inevitable? Do you believe they are "part of *normal, healthy* growth"?

3. What present or past crises have you had, and how have they affected your faith?

4. Are there some "little crises" siphoning away spiritual vitality from your life that you would care to share with others?

5. Do you think all Christians have to go through a crisis of reevaluating their faith? Have you? If so describe.

6. Do you think Christians have trouble "truth-telling"? Explain.

7. What are the "nonacceptable" crises in your community?

Experiencing God's Love and Grace This Week

Prayerfully consider the difficult situations or crises that you have had to deal with during your lifetime. Start with your earliest memories and continue to the present. Review in your mind or on paper what caused the crisis, how you handled it, and where you sensed God to be as you went through the difficulty. What have you learned from what you have gone through? Are you able to use what you have learned to help others?

Have you ever reevaluated your faith? If there is some unfinished work in this arena of your life, commit it to God and ask that in the next few weeks he would help you work through the issues in a God-glorifying way.

13

The Exchanged Life

Stage 6: Cultivating a deep trust and rest in Christ

John, a highly respected, successful surgeon in Kentucky sat at his desk with thoughts of suicide flashing through his mind. He was a dedicated Christian but struggled with a besetting sin that he couldn't seem to master. Not long after this, he was exposed to Christians who taught that one's life in Christ meant that the work was finished. Believers are kept by God's power. All he needed to do was rest in Christ. The surgeon experienced a new revelation of this old truth, which revolutionized his life. In his case he believed God wanted him to give his practice away and minister in Africa—which he did. In fact, he was the instrument God used to raise significant funds and medical equipment to start two hospitals in Tanzania and Kenya. However, his passion became sharing the phenomenal truth that our lives are complete in Christ and that he dwells within us. For a decade John has been experiencing and sharing this wonderful truth of Christ living in him.

An Epiphany Experience

When I was about 30 years old, I read my wife's copy of *Hudson Taylor's Spiritual Secret* and thought, *That's nice.* Normally when I read a book I note my impression on its pages, but there were none. I know I was impressed with his missionary zeal, but beyond that, his thoughts didn't penetrate my heart. About 35 years later I was looking over some of our books and I mused, "What was Hudson Taylor's spiritual secret?" Unable to answer that question, I picked up the book, reread it, and had an "aha" experience that propelled me to further growth. This time it came alive! Taylor's experience spoke to my heart; it was invigorating. There was an outflow of "living water." The truths he shared invaded my soul.

Usually the "Exchanged Life" is discovered through an epiphany experience. In my case I had struggled for a long time in my Christian life trying to please God. This set the stage so that the Holy Spirit could illuminate my understanding when I reread *Hudson Taylor's Spiritual Secret*. The sense that I needed to strive to please God, and to clock in a certain amount of time with him, ceased to be primary issues. I no longer relied on my Christian activity, but trusted and rested on the faithful one. Verses that I had memorized decades earlier such as "I chose you" and "Christ lives in me" (John 15:16; Galatians 2:20), I now grasped emotionally. This culminated with a paradigm shift: a looking at all of life from a different perspective—through a new set of glasses. I didn't need to reach out to God; he already was reaching out to me and actually abiding in me. I just needed to embrace this reality as fact—to make it experientially mine. This was not a new thought but a new *awareness*—an appreciation of a truth I had known cognitively but had not experienced emotionally. This lifted a giant load off me. This moment of clarity was an epiphany experience—a revelation from God. Though the specifics vary with each individual, many believers down through the ages have had such an experience.

What Was Hudson Taylor's Spiritual Secret?

So who was Hudson Taylor, and what was his profound spiritual secret? Hudson Taylor was born in England in 1832. After medical training, he went to China as a missionary in 1853. For the next 52 years, he dedicated himself in service to the Lord and to the Chinese people. He founded the China Inland Mission. His zeal for God was impressive. It seems quite clear that he was greatly influenced by Brother Lawrence: He endeavored to practice the presence of the Lord. But instead of victory, he felt defeat. Taylor experienced a constant falling short of what he thought he should be achieving despite his tenacious striving to please God. Occasionally he sensed an intimate communion with God, but most of the time, despite his best efforts, he failed. He felt ingratitude and guilt for not living closer to God, so he prayed and agonized all the more, only to end up defeated. He knew that if he could "abide in Christ," all would be well, but how to do this eluded him. He would start the day determined to remain in constant communion with God, only to be overwhelmed with the numerous pressures of the day. He describes praying, fasting, and making resolutions to no benefit. He said that instead of growing stronger, he seemed to be getting weaker with less power against sin. He cried out to "Abba, Father," seemingly to no avail.

Then after he had struggled on the mission field for *19 years,* he discovered what he called the "Exchanged Life." It was "No longer I," but rather the reality of "Christ living in me" that gave him joy and peace. Hudson Taylor discovered blessed trust and rest in the faithful one—Christ. Instead of trying to stir up faith, he now relaxed and relied on the faithful one. Instead of striving to abide in Christ, he now accepted the fact that Christ *was,* in fact, abiding in him. Communion with God became a reality.

Instead of feeling bondage, failure, and fear, he experienced a restful sense of sufficiency in Christ.

A colleague observed a remarkable change. Though Mr. Taylor's workload remained heavy, he experienced a new joy and an experiential awareness of God that made all the difference in the world. The change was so phenomenal that it seemed that he could never do enough to help others comprehend his newfound secret.[1]

Years later he was asked, " 'But are you always conscious of abiding in Christ?' He replied, 'While sleeping last night, did I cease to abide in your home because I was unconscious of the fact?' " The marvelous truth is that as new creatures in Christ, we are abiding in him, and he in us, whether we are conscious of it or not. Taylor went on to say, "We should never be conscious of not abiding in Christ."[2]

What Is the Exchanged Life?

Christ in Me

The essence of the Exchanged Life is that instead of "Dwight in Me" it is "Christ in me." We Christians have become new creatures in Christ (2 Corinthians 5:17). As new creatures, the Bible teaches, Christ abides in us (John 15:3-5). In Galatians 2:20, Paul says, "It is no longer I who live, but Christ lives in me." In fact, this is "the mystery which has been hidden…but has now been manifested…which is *Christ in you*, the hope of glory" (Colossians 1:26-27). Stop and contemplate the magnitude of this truth. The awareness of this reality can (and should) transform our lives. Instead of our working hard to please God, we are resting in the completed work of Christ. This is a life of trusting God. It isn't merely a changed life, but an *exchanged life!*

A New Heart

For a moment, picture a man suffering from heart failure. You see him struggle into a restaurant pulling a green tank of oxygen with a clear plastic tube that runs to the man's nose. His life depends on the life-giving oxygen he receives from his portable container. Every step is an effort, but without the oxygen every step is impossible. Actually, he needs a heart transplant. This is a picture of the *Christian* who is working hard to please God on his own instead of trusting in the one who offers his life-giving strength.

The person without Christ has a heart that is "deceitful above all things, and desperately wicked" (Jeremiah 17:9 KJV). The Scriptures later say, "I will give you a new heart and put a new spirit within you; and I will remove the heart of stone…and give you a heart of flesh. I will put My Spirit within you and cause you to walk in My statutes" (Ezekiel 36:25-27). This is the basis for the exchanged life. God has given us new hearts.

Sometimes after a patient has been given a new heart, the body tries to reject this life-saving organ. This drastically impairs the functioning of the implanted heart. Likewise, believers can unconsciously reject the new heart that God has so graciously given us and greatly compromise its manifest effectiveness in our lives. Spiritually, our lives compare with the patient whose life depends entirely on someone else's heart to be vibrant and meaningful. When we grasp the fact that God has given us a new heart, our whole outlook on life changes. There will be a spring in our step and we will not be as prone to sin because he has also given us a new nature. I am not denying that we have our "flesh" to deal with or saying that we can't sin. (We'll discuss that later.) But for now, it's crucial to see that God has given us a new heart and thus a new identity.

A New Identity

Being new creatures in Christ, deity in the person of the Holy Spirit dwells within us. This gives us a new identity, like when we are physically born into a family through no effort of our own, our position in the family is inherited through birth. In the same way we have been born into God's family. We are the sons and daughters of God! Using an analogy from the computer age: We've been given a password that gives us access to innumerable programs and God's bank account. This is truly mind boggling. The awareness of this reality can and should transform our lives. God wants our grasp on this truth and its significance *to radically change our concept about ourselves.* John Eldredge addresses this fact in *Waking the Dead:*

> There is a widespread belief among Christians today that the heart is desperately wicked—even after a person comes to Christ. It is a crippling belief. And it is untrue....You have a new heart. Your heart is good. That sinful nature you battle is not who you are. Twice, in the famous chapter of Romans 7, where Paul presents a first-person angst about our battle against sin, he says, "But this is not my true nature. This is not my heart."[3]

Satan has been a master at identity theft long before the computer age invented the term, and we idly sit by and allow it. When our identity is stolen, it's harder to regain than if a computer hacker steals it. In both instances, our identity may be in the hands of a thief for a long time with devastating consequences...without our even realizing it.

When our identity is stolen, we view ourselves as prone to wrongdoing, so we try managing our sin. But our focus is wrong. No matter how hard we try, life will be a continual struggle and will end in defeat. Thus Satan has not only stolen our identity but also instilled within us the false belief that we are, at the core of our lives, bad. With such a belief it is impossible to rise above a Romans 7 experience—trying to please God on our efforts and experiencing repeated failures. We have effectively rejected the new heart transplant and our identity that God has so graciously given us, and therefore we are unable to reap its full benefits.

Added to all of this is the gigantic mistake that permeated the previous generation. It's the notion that if you praise kids it will go to their heads. Parents tended to censor praise and give children plenty of criticism. As a psychiatrist I am very aware that if you criticize a child a lot, you will grease the skids for him to become a bad kid. On the other hand, if you endorse children, they tend to grow into what you communicate to them. Satan knows this only too well, so he constantly tells the person in Christ how bad he is.

Maybe you are part of the younger generation that received a lot of affirmation as you grew up; nevertheless, you may have been exposed to Christian leaders who communicated how, in the final analysis, you really don't measure up. This is often done with guilt-laden messages that tell you to do more for the Lord in hopes it will spur you on to living a productive, holy, Christian life—but it may just leave you full of holes. Satan, the accuser of the brethren, loves this and reinforces the guilt any chance he gets. Unfortunately, most of the Christian community uses guilt as the primary motivator, so we live our Christian lives feeling we are not measuring up. In contrast, God says we are his beloved, and we have a new, exchanged, transformed, transplanted heart and life with Christ in the very center. This is the great news of the gospel—and it starts right now! The exchanged life means learning by faith to embrace this truth and make it a functional reality for ourselves. Sure, we need to live it out—like the ongoing maintenance and monitoring crucial for the survival of a heart transplant patient. But our *view of ourselves* is crucial. *We have a new heart and with it a new identity!*

Recently, a group of us were discussing this chapter at a men's breakfast. Mike, a wonderful friend of mine who is Hispanic, shared the following story he rarely tells. He literally grew up on the streets of Los Angeles, often not knowing where he would sleep. When he attended school, it was in remedial classes. His mother died when he was 11 years old. At her funeral, a friend shared that Mike's mother had said she believed one of her sons "had the guts to go to college and make something of himself." (Actually, the language used was cruder.) At that moment, Mike believed it was he. Today Mike has several graduate degrees and is a consultant around the world in his field of specialty. He believed and embraced something that had been true about him all along. Embracing the belief enabled him to live it out. He started behaving as he perceived himself to be. As believers we often say "Christ is in us," but do we actually believe it? If we do, it will transform our lives. If we don't, even though it is true, we will continue to struggle in spiritual remedial classes the rest of our lives.

Trust Is Foundational

This chapter could be subtitled "The Life of Faith" because the exchanged life is primarily and foremost a life of faith. Christ said that the "work of God" is to "believe" (John 6:29). The primary *attribute* God looks for in us is our belief in him. Paul prays for his readers "that Christ may dwell in your hearts *through faith*" (Ephesians 3:17). All that is ours is received by faith. The foundational attribute is faith. This is what transformed the saints in the Scriptures. "For what does the Scripture say? 'Abraham

believed God, and it was reckoned to him as righteousness'"
(Romans 4:3). But we need a proper understanding of the nature
of this faith. Often we equate faith with a set of doctrines that one
believes. But this does not capture the essence of the faith we are
describing. Faith is not just the cognitive knowledge even the
demons have. The faith that God desires is intellectual belief and
a trust of one's total self to God. Trust indicates a reliance on and
a continual commitment to Jesus as the means to live out the
Christian life. It is not a one-time deal, but a continuous looking
in faith to our triune God.

To better communicate the nature of this faith, I like the story
of the "The Great Blondin" who, in 1859, walked across Niagara
Falls on a tightrope. He not only walked across the falls, he did a
somersault, sat down and had a drink, cooked an omelet, and rode
a bicycle on the tightrope. Then he traversed the wire and pushed
a wheelbarrow in front of him. Next he asked the crowd if they
believed he could perform this feat with a person in the wheelbarrow. Many in the crowd wholeheartedly affirmed that he
could. Then he pointed to one such individual and asked him to
get into the wheelbarrow. Though many believed he could successfully traverse the wire with someone in the wheelbarrow, none
was willing to risk his life. This vividly points out the difference
between an intellectual belief versus a personal trust. They had
faith—but not trust. The faith that we are talking about is a trust
that is willing to risk one's life for what one believes.[4] The kind
that is willing to get into the wheelbarrow!

The entire eleventh chapter of Hebrews (known as the "Hall
of Faith") illustrates this point by describing the actions some of
the outstanding men and women of the Old Testament took as a
result of their faith. Hebrews 11:1 calls faith an assurance or con-
viction. Romans 4 speaks of Abraham's faith as "being fully

assured that what God had promised, He was able also to perform" (verse 21). The faith described in these passages is an absolute reliance on God. Such a faith depends not only on the finished work of Christ for our initial salvation, but also for the living out of that righteousness in the process of becoming more and more like Christ (often called sanctification). This ongoing trust is what releases God's transforming power in our lives.

"Faithing" God's Pleasure

In chapter 1 I discussed many verses in the Scriptures that talk about our living lives that are pleasing to God. One such passage is Ephesians 5:10, which admonishes that we should "learn what is pleasing to the Lord." *The Message* elaborates: "Figure out what will please Christ, and then do it." The question then arises, "How do we please God?" So often this degenerates to our working hard to please God—to earn his pleasure. "Earning God's pleasure" is, in fact, an oxymoron. It's like "Earning our salvation." To think we can earn our salvation is an anathema to God. Likewise, to think we can earn God's favor by our works is an affront to him.

However, as with salvation, there is something we must do to receive his gracious gift of eternal life. We receive it by faith—and that is exactly the way we possess our new identity in Christ and experience the Exchanged Life. It is all through faith—a trusting, embracing faith. This is how the believer pleases God. Hebrews 11:6 makes it exceedingly clear that "without faith it is impossible to please Him." Faith then is the key and necessary avenue in contrast to "earning God's pleasure" by all the good works that we might perform. That faith however, by definition, must be active. It's not an intellectual knowledge or belief, which is a noun: one's faith = what one believes. Instead, the faith that pleases God is a verb. The Greek root word for "faith" not only has a noun form, but also a verb form, which English does not. The Bible speaks of a person "faithing in God." Therefore I am taking the liberty of using the English word "faith" as a verb to drive home the biblical truth that the only way we please God is by an *active* faith in him: *faithing God's pleasure.* James W. Fowler, in *Stages of Faith,* points out that "faith is always *relational; there is always another* [person] in faith. 'I trust *in* and am loyal *to.*'"[5] Thus the only way to please God is by an active faith dependent on God—period.

The crucial element of the exchanged life is that trust continually permeates our lives and that an ongoing reliance on the trustworthy one characterizes every aspect of our being. Hudson Taylor explains this as "resting in the Faithful One." A.W. Tozer elaborates: "Faith is occupied with the Object upon which it rests and pays no attention to itself at all....The man who has struggled to purify himself and has had nothing but repeated failures will experience real relief when he stops tinkering with his soul and looks away to the perfect One."[6]

This is why "sin management," which focuses on trying not to sin, generally leads to trying to purify the old nature by self-effort. This not only won't work, but it often causes one to sin more. However, when we focus on Christ and accept the fact that he has given us a new heart, we not only don't want to sin, but we have the means and motivation not to sin. Simply put: We either rely on ourselves to live the Christian life or we rely on Christ to live it through us. This is the crux of the life of faith or the exchanged life. It is God working in our lives to form Christ in us.

Fostering Christ Consciousness

In chapter 11 I discussed how meaningful it was to discover "practicing the presence of God." It helped direct my thoughts away from the things of the world and to focus my attention on God. At the time I didn't notice that the predominant emphasis was on God. However, as time has passed, particularly as I have become aware of the exchanged life, I have become increasingly mindful of the need and desire not only to focus on God but to also focus on Christ. This takes my relationship with the triune God and the awareness that Christ is in me to a new spiritual level. To, so to speak, "practice the presence of Christ."

So how does one foster Christ consciousness? First, there is a deliberate intent to be mindful of Christ in all areas of life. Thus, when issues at hand don't demand my attention, my mind would naturally focus on Christ. Promoting Christ consciousness must be intentional on my part. It is being aware that Christ is in me, that he has given me a new heart and identity. Furthermore, there is a sensitivity to manifestations of Christ in the world around me. All of this elevates my faith to a new plateau of living.

Receptivity

Earlier in my walk with God I took to heart passages on stirring myself up to seek God. In Stage 6—the Exchanged Life— it dawned on me in greater awareness that all along God was the active pursuer and I just needed to be receptive. I didn't need to *strive* to seek him, but I did need to intentionally respond to him.

Receptivity is an integral part of living a life of faith. Once we have initially responded to God's call on our lives, the degree to which that can be realized depends on our ongoing receptivity to God's continuous initiative toward us.[7] A.W. Tozer comments on receptivity:

> Why do some persons "find" God in a way that others do not? Why does God manifest His Presence to some and let multitudes of others struggle along in the half-light of imperfect Christian experience?...I venture to suggest that the

one vital quality which they had in common was *spiritual receptivity*....They had spiritual awareness that they went on to cultivate until it became the biggest thing in their lives.They differed from the average person in that when they felt the inward longing *they did something about it.* They acquired the lifelong habit of spiritual response....It is a gift of God, indeed, but one which must be recognized and cultivated as any other gift if it is to realize the purpose for which it was given....We will know Him in increasing degree as our receptivity becomes more perfect by faith and love and practice.[8]

Does God Possess Us?

To allow Christ free reign to live in our lives can be costly. It means yielding control to him. It means actively yielding our lives, ambitions, and reputation—everything we have—to him. Watchman Nee, who also writes on the exchanged life, says: "I must first have the sense of God's possession of me before I can have the sense of his presence with me. When once his ownership is established, then I dare do nothing in my own interests, for I am his exclusive property."[9]

He goes on to rhetorically ask, "What is the normal Christian life?" His answer is that "it is something very different from the life of the average Christian....May the Lord bring each of us to a definite issue regarding the question of his Lordship."[10] Hudson Taylor said that for him the exchanged life involved a fuller surrender—a self-abandonment to Christ.

Results of the Exchanged Life

An Adventure

Embarking up the trail of the Exchanged Life—*a journey from whom you have been, to whom you are*—is both a sacrifice and an adventure. It is a *sacrifice* because you have to give up the predictable, black-and-white, concrete road markers and well-paved streets of a Stage 2 life (knowing God's truths and doing them) that have become so familiar. These markers, even if they become threadbare, have become like a security blanket, and our tendency is to fight anyone who would take them from us. *It is an adventure* because "the life of faith" is much less predictable; you are trailblazing into uncharted areas with Christ as your guide.

My daughter tells a wonderful story along this line. While in high school she and her brother were skiing in the Utah mountains on a very foggy day with visibility of about 30 feet. They never would have attempted to ski that day on their own. But a personal friend who was on the ski patrol and knew the mountain well offered to take them skiing. Susan and Greg didn't need to know where they were going. They only had to keep their eyes on him and follow closely behind. Susan had more fun skiing that day than on any other day because it was an adventure. She knew that no matter what happened, their guide knew what to do. The life of faith is a life of adventure following close after Christ, keeping our gaze always on him.

It's a Life of Rest—The Right Kind of Rest

"So there is a special rest still waiting for the people of God. For all who enter into God's rest will find rest from their labors, just as God rested after creating the world. Let us do our best to enter that place of rest" (Hebrews 4:9-11 NLT). The King James Bible renders verse 11: "Let us labour therefore to enter into that rest." Labor to enter into rest sounds like an oxymoron—but it isn't. The best analogy that comes to my mind is that of floating on water. People afraid of drowning often thrash about, wear themselves out, and may even fight with their rescuers. But there is another option that is altogether counterintuitive. Instead of fighting the water or the rescuer, the person gives himself to the water by lying on his back and allowing the water to come up to the edge of his nose. With *trust,* you can gently lie with your head back and rely on the buoyancy of the water to hold you up—and it does. Likewise, our frantic works to master sin and to produce for God will only change the mode of operation to a works orientation, and we will fail to rest in Christ. If, on the other hand, we will rest in our Savior, he will sustain us. Our part is to rely on him; his part is to hold us up. The exchanged life is a life of faith, characterized by resting in Christ.

Abundant Life

I believe living the exchanged life, along with what we will be talking about in the next chapter is the epitome of the abundant life. And that is the very life that God wants you and me to have. He said: "I came that they may have life, and may have it abundantly" (John 10:10).

The Pyramid of Spiritual Growth

We are now ready to add our sixth tier to our Pyramid of Spiritual Growth (*Illustration 8*) "The Exchanged Life (Faithing)."

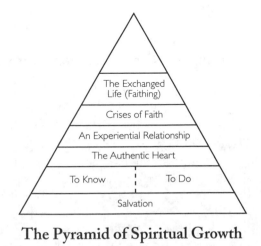

The Pyramid of Spiritual Growth

Illustration 8

Discussion Questions

1. How do you think deeply believing Christ lives in you would affect your life?

2. How would you explain to someone what the "exchanged life" is all about?

3. Have you had an epiphany experience in your walk with Christ? Describe.

4. Do you personally think Christians have good or bad hearts? What are the implications of your answer?

5. Do you think Christian leaders are afraid to tell us we have good hearts? If so, why?

6. What do you think of the distinction the author makes between faith and trust?

7. What do you think about the concept of "fostering Christ consciousness"?

Experiencing God's Love and Grace This Week

Make a conscious effort to remember that Christ actually lives in you in the person of the Holy Spirit and that God has given you a new, good heart. Try and return to this thought many times. Meditate on Galatians 2:20; Colossians 1:25-27; and Philippians 1:21. You may want to mark them in your Bible and memorize these verses if you haven't done so already.

If you have not read Hudson Taylor's Spiritual Secret (Chicago: Moody Press, 1932), I urge you to obtain a copy of this small paperback and read chapter 14, "The Exchanged Life."

14

The Life of Adoration

Stage 7: Realizing and responding
to God's profound love

"Pssssssssss—tssssss…psssssssssss—tssssss." Hour after hour the respirator hissed on. "Pssssssssss—tssssss…" Meryl's life depended completely upon that machine. She lay in ICU mentally alert yet completely paralyzed. A few days earlier she had been in perfect health; now she lay stricken with an illness whose name she had never heard: Guillain-Barre Disease. The first three weeks, when she couldn't communicate at all, were the worst. But it was during this period of time that she became acutely aware of God's presence and love. He seemed to be talking to her.[1]

It was as if God wanted to get her attention. First, she felt him assuring her, saying, "Don't be afraid. You're going through some rough times now, but I want to talk to you. You've had enough hurts in the past. You are going to be okay. I want you to trust me." And so Meryl did.

Then she became aware of one message over and over again: "Meryl, I love you." Though Meryl was a faithful churchgoer, she wasn't convinced that God loved her. She argued with God: "But I don't do all that I'm supposed to. I don't read my Bible enough.

I don't witness." And the voice came back to her again saying, "It's okay, Meryl. I love you. I understand." Then she protested: "But I'm the girl who always was ripping the pocket off my dress—everything seemed to break as soon as I touched it. All my dolls had broken arms, and their heads were on sideways."

Then the anguish of the past started to surface. One of Meryl's children had been born with severe neurological and mental problems and finally had to be institutionalized. "Why, God—Why?" she cried out. "Why did you let my son go through this pain?" And to all this outpouring God simply replied, "I love you, and I love your son. You are very special to me."

Meryl was dependent on that respirator for more than two months and was hospitalized for almost three months. Except for a slight speech difficulty, she recovered and returned to teaching. Now she is able to look back and say, "I can see that God really was guiding me all my life, even though there were times when I thought he didn't hear me or didn't understand. He was just waiting for his time to talk to me. God was very, very close during my illness. I felt his complete acceptance of me. I am singularly blessed in having had those weeks with the Lord."

Through this severe illness—this crisis of faith—Meryl gained an entirely new outlook upon life. She now realizes that she is a special person whom God deeply loves despite her human frailties.

Love Is Crucial

Love is a recurring theme throughout the Scriptures. Paul realized the importance of love and devotes almost half of the book of Ephesians to this important subject. In 1 Corinthians he moves to a crescendo saying, "And now abide faith, hope, love, these three; but the greatest of these is love" (1 Corinthians 13:13 NKJV).

Love is the one thing that can satisfy the deep longings of our hearts. The authors of *The Sacred Romance* say "the heart-cry of every soul [is] for intimacy with God. For this we were created and for this we were rescued from sin and death....In the end, all we've ever really wanted is to be loved."[2]

All true love starts with God. Love connects us to God and people. It transforms lives. It is one of the most powerful forces in the world. David Benner says in *Surrender to Love*, "It is the experience of love that is transformational. You simply cannot bask in divine love and not be affected."[3] Love can transform the unbeliever or the legalistic, performance-based, judgmental Christian into gracious followers of Christ.

Receiving and Giving Love

To receive and give love is one of the hardest—if not *the* hardest—task we human beings have to master. Many people, if not most, never succeed. Oh, we have countless songs about love in every type of music known on earth, but most of that is about selfish *eros* love. We know about *phileo*, friendship love, but even that has its limits.

To truly receive love without any strings attached, *agape* love, and to give such love, is a very rare commodity, even among Christians. Sure, Christians know that "God loves you and has a wonderful plan for your life" and that "God so loved the world." But for most of us, it is a cognitive knowledge that hasn't deeply penetrated our souls. There may have been a brief overwhelming sense of God's love when we originally came to him, but for so many, that is long gone. David Benner comments, "Talking about such a [love] relationship is easy. Actually coming to develop a love relationship with the invisible God is far from simple. It doesn't happen automatically for anyone."[4]

Psychoanalytic psychiatry considers love to be the epitome of emotional maturity. I believe that when a person truly receives God's love, especially in an ongoing way, and responds to God in love, he or she is at the apex of spiritual maturity. Love is what we crave more than anything else, whether we recognize it or not.

Why is it so hard to receive and give love? There are many reasons, but here are some major ones.

We Don't Recognize Our True Need

If we want and need love so badly, why is it so difficult to receive? First of all, we don't recognize that love is what we are missing. We think pleasure, sex, power, wealth, or the praise of others will satisfy the deep longings of our hearts. We strive for these without realizing that it is love we are missing.

Love Violates Our Intuitive Notion of "Earning"

Receiving God's no-strings-attached love violates our intuitive rules about earning and achievement. We want to get our act together in order to deserve love—and that is what will interfere with our ability to receive his love. In fact, both trust and love violate our deeply embedded sense of earning. Since we were knee-high to a grasshopper we have been taught we must eat our broccoli before we get dessert. Strange as it may seem, we are more comfortable knowing we've *earned* something because then we have a "right" to it and can claim the credit for it. We want to come to God as worthy rather than just as we are—warts and all. God wants us to come to him as needy people, empty handed, embracing the gift of his love and grace. Christ exemplified this as he welcomed sinners with open arms. They came without pretense—just as they were—much to the dismay of the religious and morally "upright" of his day.

Coming Naked

Adam and Eve walked with God fully exposed and without embarrassment until they sinned—then they hid. God called them to come out from their hiding places just as they were—naked (though trying to hide it with fig leaves). Only then did *he* clothe them. You and I, without God, are ashamed of who we are. We, apart from God's Spirit, want to correct our shortcomings first and then come to God. God wants us to come to him just as we are, and then he will cover us with his righteousness. This is the essence of his grace. If we hide anything, we hide from God. Only as we accept our own nakedness and shame and realize he accepts us as we are will we be in a position to fully take in and act on his love. Such transparency is essential, not only initially, but also in our ongoing relationship with Christ. For God to transform our lives, we must continue to live with transparent openness and vulnerability at the core of our relationship with him.

Developmental Wounds

For many people, a factor that complicates their relationship with God is the fact that when they were young, the important people (such as parents and teachers) in their lives communicated that they didn't measure up. They got the message that in the final analysis they weren't loveable. Christianity has often added to such wounds as these individuals are very sensitive to anything that is guilt inducing. I know of situations where sensitive individuals have left a service deeply injured by the comments of a leader, and yet I have heard from others attending the same service, "Wasn't that great—we need more hard-hitting messages like that." The point is that in this arena, the thickness of our skin, so to speak, varies greatly. Some individuals don't feel guilt or change their behavior when hit by a two-by-four, while the person sitting in the next pew may be shattered.

Satan's Lies

On top of all of this, Satan, the Deceiver, will do everything in his power to steal our hearts and destroy our belief that God truly loves us. C. Baxter Kruger, in the *Parable of the Dancing God*, says, "[Satan] is a rejection specialist, and his chief strategy is to convince us that we are not acceptable....If he can convince us that God has rejected us, or even that God does not like us or want us, then the game of life is up. We become like the ten-year-old girl sitting in her room in tears. When we do venture out, we do so as wounded people."[5]

The Depth of God's Love

But God deeply loves you and me. His love is unconditional, and he wants us to receive it as a gift. He loves us with an ever-lasting love that is as high as the heavens are above the earth, and he wants us to be able to feel and understand and experience this love for ourselves (see Jeremiah 31:3; Psalm 103:11; Ephesians 3:18-19). The Scriptures overflow with examples that show us how much God loves us. In fact, *he loves you and me as much as he loves his only begotten Son, Jesus Christ,* according to John 17:23. What an amazing, unfathomable truth about God's love!

Basking in God's Love

How do we receive God's love? How do we deeply absorb the reality that he loves us? For a moment, picture people on the seashore basking in the sun. They aren't doing anything to deserve or create the sun, but they purposefully expose themselves to the warm rays. The dictionary defines bask: "To lie in or be exposed to a pleasant warmth: to bask in the sun. To take great pleasure; revel; to bask in royal favor."[6]

Receiving God's love requires uninhibited exposure to the *Son*. God's Word is the key means by which he radiates his truths to us. Surrendering ourselves to God is another essential element in exposing ourselves to him. We also need sufficient relaxed time to allow the rays to penetrate and to listen to the still, small voice of the Holy Spirit speaking to our hearts and minds. Often this learning to receive God's love is both a process and, sometimes, an epiphany experience at one or several points on our spiritual journey.

At some level, I have been aware of God's love for me from the day I accepted Christ many years ago. When I became aware that God wanted an experiential relationship with me (Stage 4), the sense of that love increased. But entering into this seventh stage of growth, which has taken place in my 60s, has given me a much greater realization of the profound love God has for me. This has come as I have been reading through the Scriptures repeatedly over the last half dozen years, looking for the loving, personal interaction of the triune God with his people. At the same time, I have been reading numerous books along these lines. It's been dawning on me the depth of God's love for me and that he actually wants an intimate relationship with me.

God Wants a Romance with You!

Philip Yancey says what God has been seeking all along with the human race is "the mature, freely given love of a lover. He has been 'romancing' us all along."[7] Brent Curtis and John Eldredge develop this truth throughout their excellent book *The Sacred Romance: Drawing Closer to the Heart of God*.[8] To be honest with you, the title of the book initially offended me. It sounded sensual, even sexual, and for many sensuality has not only been foreign, but antithetical to spirituality—if not frankly offensive. But ultimately God used this book and some others, along with the Scriptures, to touch my heart and ignite a sense of romance with God, a divine love relationship.

Romance Requires Surrender

To enter into a romance with God requires surrender. I talked about surrender in chapter 12—typified by surrender of a defeated army or a person's accepting a terminal illness when there is no other option. To enter into a romance with God requires not only surrender but also being sensitive to the wishes of the one loved—a total giving of oneself for the pleasure of the other. That is the essence of the romance God wants with us. David Benner says, "Christian obedience should always be based on surrender to a person....It is surrender to love, not submission to a duty.... Christian obedience is more like what lovers give each other than what soldiers give their superiors. Lovers demonstrate their love by doing what each other wants."[9]

Furthermore, when we fall in love with the awesome creator of the universe, realizing who he is, we will fall on our knees to worship him. For he desires a called-out people who will be responsive to him—to not only love him, but also to worship him.

Worship

Christ declared, "But an hour is coming, and now is, when the true worshipers will worship the Father in spirit and truth; *for such people the Father seeks to be His worshipers.* God is spirit, and those who worship Him must worship in spirit and truth" (John 4:23-24). Kent Hughes says, "That the Father *seeks* worshipers is unparalleled, for nowhere in the entire corpus of Holy Scripture do we read of God's seeking anything else from a child of God. *God desires worship above all else.*[10]

Oswald Chambers asserts, "Worshiping God is the great essential of [spiritual] fitness."[11] Tozer adds, "God saves men to make them worshipers....It may be set down as an axiom that if we do not worship we cannot work acceptably....Without doubt the emphasis in Christian teaching today should be on worship. There is little danger that we shall become merely worshipers and neglect the practical implications of the gospel."[12] Kent Hughes likewise affirms, "Worship is the number one priority of the church." He goes on to say:

> A look at the massive emphasis on worship in the Old Testament reveals God's mind on worship's priority. Exodus devotes twenty-five chapters to the construction of the Tabernacle, the locus of divine worship. Leviticus amounts to a twenty-seven chapter liturgical manual. And the Psalms are a spectacular 150-chapter worship hymnal. Divine worship has always been the occupation and sustenance, the priority, of the believing soul.[13]

Heaven will be characterized by worship. Revelation 7:9-11 KJV says, "A great multitude, which no man could number, of all nations, and kindreds, and people, and tongues...worshipped God." The whole work of redemption will find its culmination in men and women who have been fitted to worship God.

What is worship? It is often described as speaking to God of his worth, delighting to reflect his worth back to him. When combining Hebrew and Greek words, worship has been defined as "an inner and outer homage to God as a token of awe and surrender" and "a total lifestyle in allegiance to God."[14] Worship is all about God.

Love + Worship = Adoration

I believe God has an intense desire that we love *and* worship him—that we adore him. Webster defines *adore* as "to regard with the utmost esteem, love, and respect. To pay divine honor, to worship" and *adoration* is described as "the act of paying honor, as to a divine being; worship, reverent homage, fervent and devoted love."[15] As I read the Scriptures, it seems very apparent to me that in addition to trust, the two attributes that God wants most from us—his creation—is our genuine love and worship.

How Do You Adore God?

If adoring God is so important—how do we do it? Part of me would like to give you "five easy steps" to accomplish this, but we must be very careful here. I could very easily make this a "to do" list and put us right back in the Stage 2 of growth. Numerous biblical passages emphasize the manifestations of love in our lives. Yet, we again must be careful as we can focus on activities that can be mimicked without an authentic heart attitude of love. Likewise, we could describe outward forms of worship and miss the heart of worship. There is an aspect of all this that defies definition, quantification, or analysis. The hallmark of love and worship is a *heart attitude* of adoration.

I also find it hard to tell you how to adore God because I am a novice in this arena, learning myself how to love and worship our wonderful Lord. But perhaps that can be an encouragement to you: we are never too old to begin learning how to receive God's love and respond to him in love and worship. A person often feels rather foolish when in love, but Scripture speaks of coming to God like little children, who know how to unabashedly love and adore people.

Having said this, I do think some general ideas on this subject can be articulated. Most of us remember falling in love and how that felt. We repeatedly thought about the one we loved during any free minutes and used any excuse to call and talk to our love. We looked forward to just being with him or her. We looked at the person with admiration and a heartfelt feeling of affirmation and warmth. And we would never want to do anything to disappoint or hurt our loved one. In adoring God, there will be these same attitudes and feelings. In addition, there will be a sense of awe and reverence that goes beyond just thinking about God; there will be a heart full of love, worship, and praise to the Father, Son, and Holy Spirit.

I personally have noticed a greater sense of gratitude and praise to God—accompanied with a love and appreciation for him that wells up within me. Paul describes and encourages us to "let the word of Christ dwell in you richly...as you sing psalms, hymns and spiritual songs with gratitude in your hearts to God" (Colossians 3:16 NIV).

The Ultimate Aim: To Glorify God

As we live lives characterized by trust and adoration of God, we will be glorifying God, which should be the ultimate aim of our lives. The more mature we are in Christ, the more this will be the inevitable fruit of our lives. As we carefully read through the Scriptures, it's clear that the purpose of all creation is to bring glory to God. The psalmist declares, "The heavens are telling of the glory of God; and their expanse is declaring the work of His hands" (Psalm 19:1). The cry of Christ's heart was "Father, glorify Your name"; thus, he could say, "God is glorified in [me]" (John 12:28; 13:31). We are told: "For you have been bought with a price: therefore glorify God in your body" (1 Corinthians 6:20).

The Westminster Catechism had it right when it declared that man's chief end is "to glorify God, and to enjoy him forever."[16]

The Pyramid of Spiritual Growth

We are now ready to complete the Pyramid of Spiritual Growth *(Illustration 9)* by adding Stage 7. Adoration, which is love and worship of God, is the apex of spiritual maturity. You will notice a dotted line between Stages 6 and 7, as I believe these two stages, trust and adoration, are inseparable and are where we need to give ongoing special attention. As we trust and adore our triune God we will, in fact, appropriately apply all the stages of growth, as we will see in the next chapter.

The Pyramid of Spiritual Growth

Illustration 9

One additional observation: The pyramid, representing our lives, points upward to God—to his glorification!

Ongoing Need for Each Stage

Throughout the book I have used the analogy of a journey and this lends itself to illustrate several important truths in our walk with God. First, that our life in Christ has a beginning and a progressive aspect to it that's comparable to a journey or the maturation of our physical bodies. Second, that obstacles occur along the way with the ever-present possibility of our getting stuck. These important concepts are very scriptural. However, this analogy does have at least one major drawback that a pyramid helps communicate.

The Pyramid of Spiritual Growth conveys the concept that no matter how mature we are in Christ, we continually need to partake of *all* the ingredients, of the "nutrients" of each stage of growth. In this respect it is like the Food Pyramid. Just as all the basic food nutrients are essential throughout our lives, so it is with the spiritual.

Though the first step of "being saved" is a one-time decision on our part, we are in fact resting on the ongoing power of God to complete the work he has begun in us until we are home with him in heaven. The rest of the stages require an ongoing, *intentional* involvement on our part, making for a nutritious spiritual diet—a mature Christian's diet.

Over time the characteristic aspects of some of these stages may take on a slightly different form. For example, early in our walk with God, Stage 2 may look quite traditional: Bible study, prayer, regular time alone with God, fellowship with other believers, and some area of ministry. As we grow in Christ, these may be lived out in slightly different ways especially as you add other "spiritual disciplines" to your life.[17]

The Stages Aren't So Neat and Linear

Joe is a "completed" Jew, and a member of our men's breakfast group. After studying the material in this book he brought in a complicated diagram depicting his spiritual journey. At first glance it reminded me of a picture of the human intestine as illustrated in *Gray's Anatomy!* He depicted a winding course and listed the stages of growth as he progressed up the trail. Then he drew what he called "shoots or slides" between the various stages. He found, at times, that he had slipped back to an earlier stage even though he didn't want to go there. He also had some tunnels where he could see ahead but somehow didn't seem to be able to arrive at the next stage. The take-home message is that there are a lot of different ways to illustrate one's pilgrimage and they are often a lot more messy than my nice looking pyramid might communicate. Furthermore, we are all unique, so some aspects of your journey will be different than mine.

Discussion Questions

1. How did you do this last week in remembering that Christ actually lives in you in the person of the Holy Spirit and that God has given you a new, good heart? Did you notice any change in your attitude or actions?

2. Do you find it harder to give or receive love? What inhibits you from absorbing all the love that God has for you?

3. Do you think work for the "kingdom" could be counterproductive if it isn't done out of a heart attitude of love and worship of God?

4. Could a person live a life of true "faith and adoration" and be deficient in some of the other stages of growth?

5. Can you see how Christians who are at one stage of growth might be prone to judge others who are at different stages of growth? Cite some examples.

6. Some writers on spiritual growth stages believe that after some individuals have experienced all the stages of growth, they tend to migrate to a "home stage"—that is, a stage in which they are most comfortable.[18] What do you think of this notion? Is it healthy? Do you have a home stage?

Experiencing God's Love and Grace This Week

You have now considered seven stages to spiritual maturity. During the next week prayerfully consider where you are on your spiritual journey—how far you have progressed and whether or not you have hit any obstacles. Chart your spiritual journey. Your diagram may look very different from the one that I have described in this book—that's O.K. You may be aware that there are vistas ahead that you have not traveled; consequently, you may want to leave that area of your pyramid or diagram blank. Be imaginative.

If you have navigated each stage, you have successfully overcome the seven major obstacles to spiritual growth. Congratulations!

If you have time you might want to read chapter 7, "The Beloved," in Brent Curtis and John Eldredge's *The Sacred Romance*.[19]

15

The Transformed Life

In the previous seven chapters, I have presented the stages that lead to a mature, transformed life. Romans 12:2 MSG speaks of this transformation as being "changed from the inside out." J.B. Phillips puts it this way: "Let God re-mould your minds from within." And in Ephesians we are told to "take on an entirely new way of life—a God-fashioned life, a life renewed from the inside and working itself into your conduct as God accurately reproduces his character in you" (Ephesians 4:22-24 MSG).

The natural result of the life in Christ will be fruit (John 15). However, a humanly capable Christian can produce a tremendous amount of "fruit" through his or her natural (fleshly) abilities. For example, King Solomon began his leadership with a heart of faith and obedience to God and built an impressive empire, including a trillion dollar gold-layered temple to God. He wowed the world but not his Maker because his work became a monument to himself. He started his reign in dependence on God but completed it through his own efforts. In contrast, there were many Old Testament prophets who had genuine faith and obedience, but humanly speaking had much less than Solomon to show for it. Thus, there can be "fruit" that is merely the result of one's personal achievements or there can be genuine fruit that grows out of a life of faith and adoration. It is the latter that we are talking about in this chapter. This is the only kind of fruit that is pleasing to the Father.

A Life Centered on Christ

A life focused on obedience is not a transformed life. It concentrates one's attention on what we are doing for God and how we are avoiding sin. As stated earlier, it specializes in behavior modification that tends to leave the heart untouched. You might call this "religious obedience." It has as its object our neighbors, good works, witnessing, and keeping certain rules, taken from the Scriptures. Such obedience has its primary focus in the wrong place and often becomes an activity of the flesh. The church at Galatia, like Solomon, began in the Spirit but then quickly reverted to "being perfected by the flesh" (Galatians 3:3). They started out in faith and quickly ended in works. It's so easy to slip into the obedience of rules. Rules can become measurable markers of spiritual success and cease to have God as their means and object.

Our focus is to be on our triune God and in particular, Christ. As we trust him with our lives and listen to the Holy Spirit as he personally and intimately directs us, then we will not only do what he wants us to do, *we will want to do* what he wants us to do. This dramatically lightens the load for the Christian—it makes his "burden light." Such obedience will always be consistent with what the Scriptures teach. This is the "obedience of faith" or the "obedience to Christ"—the *only* obedience that pleases the heart of God (Romans 1:4-5; 16:26; 2 Corinthians 10:5).

No longer will our focus be on rules or the pressure that people put on us—but on Christ. No longer is the means of achieving his purposes our clenched-teeth determination to do what is "right," but it will be the outflow of our lives in Christ. This changes our life from a "have to" to a "want to." Furthermore, it takes the ominous pressure that rules always develop and people promote off our backs. It's how God changes our lives from the inside out and gives us abundant life.

True Faith, Love, Worship, and Obedience

Authentic faith always results in obedience. Hebrews 11 describes the stalwarts in the "Hall of Faith." Their faith was verified by their actions. The major theme of the Epistle of James is that faith will manifest itself in appropriate action. It is the obedience of the person willing to get into the wheelbarrow and be pushed on a tightrope across the Niagara Falls (see chapter 13).

Loving God will also result in obedience. In John 14, Christ emphasizes this fact three times: "If you love Me, you will keep My commandments," "He who has My commandments and keeps them is the one who loves Me," and "If anyone loves Me, he will keep My word" (John 14:15,21,23). John tells us, "The proof that we love God comes when we keep his commandments" (1 John 5:3 MSG).

The truth is that if we have an obedience problem, we actually have a more basic problem of not trusting our lives to Christ and loving him. An obedienceless faith is an oxymoron; it is not possible. *The result and confirmation of trust and love is obedience.*

Additionally, *worship will lead to obedience.* When truly worshiping God, our hearts will be aligned with his heart and his will for us. The natural result is always godly action.

Faith Expressing Itself Through Love

The Scriptures teach "for in Christ Jesus neither circumcision nor uncircumcision has any value. *The only thing that counts is faith expressing itself through love*" (Galatians 5:6 NIV). For those of us without a Jewish heritage, *The Message* translates this more to the point: "For in Christ, neither our most conscientious religion nor disregard of religion amounts to anything. What matters is something far more interior: faith expressed in love."

This passage is making two powerful statements. First, as we were discussing earlier, our self-determined religious efforts amount to nothing. Some of us have worked very hard at trying to be obedient out of sheer willpower. As noble as this might seem on the surface, the motivation is wrong. David Benner wisely says:

> To rely on the will for Christian obedience is to reinforce our natural willful self-determination. This lies right at the core of our egocentricity, something that no human has to be taught....Relying on the will to make things happen keeps us focused on the self. Life lived with resolve and determination is life lived apart from surrender. It is living with clenched-fisted doggedness. It is living the illusion that I can be in control. It is the rule of life lived in the kingdom of self.
>
> Obedience that flows from a surrendered heart is totally different. Rather than willpower and resolve, love is the motive for what we will and what we do. This is the pattern of genuine Christian spiritual transformation...[which] always works from the inside out. And love is always its source, motivation and expression.[1]

The second point of Galatians 5:6 is that genuine faith in God will manifest itself by loving God and those around us. God's Word tells us, "If God so loved us, we also ought to love one another" (1 John 4:11). God is preeminently interested in a heart attitude of love. With Christ as the source and our being open conduits, that love will inevitability manifest itself in loving action toward the people around us. Our genuine love of the people in the world will verify that God's love is actually in us.

John says, "If we love one another, God abides in us, and His love is perfected in us" (1 John 4:12). Faith that is authentic results in love.

The Manifestations of Faith Through Love

The Scriptures remind us that a good tree cannot bring forth bad fruit. When the object of our faith is God, it will produce certain manifestations. You would have to comb the Scriptures from cover to cover for a complete list, but love, as defined in 1 Corinthians 13, and the fruit of the Spirit, as listed in Galatians 5:22-23, are good places to start. That brings us to another question: With maturity, will some attributes of trust and love be more evident in us?

Awareness of God's Presence

When we trust and love God, we will see Christ in our world. We will have a new outlook that sees manifestations of God's grace and presence all around us. It will be a God-saturated world. Such an outlook lends itself to gracious, spontaneous acts of kindness, concern, generosity, and a desire to cooperate with what God is already doing in the world.

A Christ-Focused, Holy Spirit-Directed Life

Galatians 2:20 says, "I have been crucified with Christ; and it is no longer I who live, but Christ lives in me; and the life which I now live in the flesh I live by faith in the Son of God, who loved me and gave Himself up for me." Christ lives in you and me. Trusting and adoring Christ *requires* that we focus on him and *results* in our focusing on him. We then will be living a *Christ-saturated, Christ-intoxicated life*. As God fills our lives, he will energize our service.

As our focus centers more and more on Christ, our moment-by-moment activities will be inspired and prompted by the Holy Spirit. Paul tells the Galatians, "Walk by the Spirit, and you will not carry out the desire of the flesh....But if you are led by the Spirit, you are not under the Law" (Galatians 5:16,18). The only way we will know how to live out our lives in Christ is with sensitivity to the Holy Spirit. The missing link that puts all this together is the Holy Spirit. If we rely on human wisdom to know when we need to take some action, we will mess up. That is the reason Christ *abides in us* and is our *helper, teacher,* and *guide* (John 14:16,26; 16:7,13).

Deliverance from the Power of Sin

Satan and the power of sin exert tremendous influence over the non-Christian. But Paul reminds us "the power of sin is the law" (1 Corinthians 15:56). Therefore, the clout of sin continues to exert incredible pressure over the Christian who lives by rules, laws, or out of the flesh. But when we are living a life of faith in and adoration of Christ, the power of Satan is crushed. In 1 Corinthians 15:57, Paul says, "But thanks be to God, who gives us the victory [over the power of sin] through our Lord Jesus Christ." And in Romans, he says, "Sin shall not be your master, because you are not under law, but under grace" (Romans 6:14 NIV).

There is a direct correlation between the extent to which God controls our lives and the degree of influence that sin has over us. Sanctification delivers us from the power of sin. Therefore, as we progress through the stages of growth the crushing grip of sin becomes weaker and weaker.

Not Prone to Sin, but Capable of Sinning

Lest I be misunderstood: As long as we are living in our earthly bodies, we will be *capable* of sinning. In his letter to Christians,

John said: "If we say that we have no sin we are deceiving ourselves" (1 John 1:8). Paul cautioned, "Therefore let him who thinks he stands take heed that he does not fall" (1 Corinthians 10:12).

The book of Galatians wonderfully tells of us of our freedom in Christ. However, in the strongly affirmative fifth chapter it says, "For you were called to freedom, brethren; only do not turn your freedom into an opportunity for the flesh" (Galatians 5:13). The more we comprehend our identity in Christ, the more revolting sin will become. *We will not want to sin.* When we are deeply in love with someone, we don't entertain the thought of doing anything that would displease him or her. Nevertheless, the Holy Spirit gently warns us, in the midst of a chapter applauding our freedom in Christ, that we are still capable of sinning.

When I think of the Christian's relationship to sin, I think of dog poop in the park. On approaching such a mess you instantly identify the smelly, revolting stuff, making sure to give it plenty of room and move on. You certainly wouldn't focus on it, but you surely would avoid it! That's the way sin will be in the transformed Christian: No denial that it's out there, but absolutely no interest in it because it's offensive, smelly stuff—especially to God, the one we love.

If we sin, it doesn't alter our sonship or daughtership. But our affective relationship with our heavenly Father is temporarily hampered by our sin. For when we sin we avoid the light and run from God's presence. We can't bask in God's love with unconfessed sin any more than Adam and Eve could freely and openly walk with God in the garden after they sinned. They hid themselves.

When I was about ten years old, my dad and I went camping in the mountains. An older boy had a car and wanted to go to a store several miles down the mountain. He invited some other boys and me to go along. I was unable to find my dad to tell him where I was going, and since I thought I would be right back I went along. But the car broke down. Hours later, at dusk, I returned to find my dad standing beside the river. He had concluded that I must have drowned. His face wore a look of deep grief, so deep it was palpable. When he saw me, he asked where I had been. I told him, telling him I was sorry. He wasn't angry with me; he only said that he wished I had told him I was leaving the area as he had walked up and down the river for hours concluding I was dead. My actions greatly affected my father.

Our actions likewise affect our heavenly Father—a truth that hundreds of verses and examples in the Scripture support. "Draw near to God and He will draw near to you" (James 4:8). God was pleased with Abel and his offering, but rejected Cain's (Genesis 4:3-7). God was grieved over the wickedness of humanity during Noah's time, but was pleased with Noah (Genesis 6:5-9). Our trusting and responding in loving obedience is exceedingly important to God, and our attitude and behavior affects his emotional response to us. Comprehension of this scriptural truth is crucial to understanding our dynamic relationship with our living Lord.

When we do sin, God doesn't want us to get bogged down because of it. He wants us to fully own it, have a contrite heart, confess it, forsake it, and forget it. Our focus needs to be on God's sinlessness, not our own sinfulness.

Owning Our Brokenness

We are all broken people. When we first come to the Lord, he accepts us as we are…and typically the church does also. But if a Stage 2, "To Know/To Do," atmosphere characterizes our Christian environment, the new convert will soon sense that it's not okay to sin and mess up. He will be expected to manage his sin. So the young Christian learns to push the sin underground, where it develops a life of its own. Hidden away, sin, emotional issues, and personal weaknesses take on altered forms and become formidable foes to deal with. Brennan Manning says:

> The great weakness in the North American church at large, and certainly in my life, is our refusal to accept our brokenness. We hide it, evade it, and gloss over it. We grab for the cosmetic kit and put on our virtuous face to make ourselves admirable to the public. Thus, we present to others a self that is spiritually together, superficially happy, and lacquered....If there is a conspicuous absence of power and wisdom in the North American church, it has arisen because we have not come to terms with the tragic flaw in our lives: the brokenness that is proper to the human condition.[2]

Transparency, an Inevitable Result

In contrast to hiding our brokenness, the mature follower of Christ who has moved into the later stages of spiritual growth will realize that he or she must become more transparent in order to continue maturing. We can't have maturity without significant transparency, and that will manifest some messiness as we discussed in chapter 10. Our brokenness becomes more apparent as we are increasingly exposed to God's light and love.

Nevertheless, the process works both ways: As we mature and become more aware of our weaknesses and brokenness, we are also learning to trust God enough to be honest about our weaknesses, which enables his love to bring about a lot of healing and growth.

Attitude About Personal Desires

As we mature in our trust and love of God, a personal agenda and our own status before others becomes less important. I appreciate so much what Dallas Willard says on this matter:

Apprentices of Jesus will be deeply disturbed about many things and will passionately desire many things, but they will be largely indifferent to the fulfillment of their own desires as such. Merely getting their way has no significance for them....They do not have to look out for themselves because God—and not they—is in charge of their life... [There will be an] abandonment of defensiveness [including] all practices of self-justification, evasiveness, and deceit, as well as manipulation....We do not hide and we do not follow strategies for "looking good."[3]

Softer and Less Dogmatic

On occasion when I have presented some of this material in lecture form, people often ask, "How are you different now than when you were in the earlier stages of growth?" One of the things I have noticed is that I know less. Oh, I have more factual information now, and I do believe I have a little more wisdom. But I am much more aware that many issues, even spiritual issues, are not as black and white as I once thought. Recently a publisher approached me about reprinting my first book written in the early 1970s.[4] I was delighted to get this book on fatigue back into print but told the publisher I would certainly want to update the scientific material and probably make other changes reflecting my own growth.[5] As I went through the book, I was amazed at how sure I was about so many things back then—how black and white it all was—and how quick I was to label some things as sin. I now know a lot more, including the limits of my knowledge and the fact that many variables enter into every situation. As a result, the updated version is stated more softly.

Brennan Manning says in *Ruthless Trust*, "When I heard an elderly and saintly friar in the monastery comment, 'The older I get, the less I understand about God,' I assumed that it was his sincere attempt at modesty. Secretly, however, I pitied his shallowness. Looking back now, I shudder at my 'profundity.'" [6] A.W. Tozer also gives us some sage advice along this line:

> Christianity is rarely found pure. Apart from Christ and His inspired apostles probably no believer or company of believers in the history of the world has ever held the truth in total purity....No believer, however pure his heart or however obedient his life, has ever been able to receive it as it shines from the Throne unmodified by *his own mental stuff*....The conclusion of the matter is that we should not assume that we have all the truth and that we are mistaken in nothing.[7]

The Holy Spirit through Paul likewise encourages us:

> Welcome with open arms fellow believers who don't see things the way you do. And don't jump all over them every time they do or say something you don't agree with—even when it seems that they are strong on opinions but weak in the faith department. Remember, they have their own history to deal with. Treat them gently....
>
> Forget about deciding what's right for each other. Here's what you need to be concerned about: that you don't get in the way of someone else, making life more difficult than it already is....
>
> So let's agree to use all our energy in getting along with each other. Help others with encouraging words; don't drag them down by finding fault....Cultivate your own relationship with God, but don't impose it on others (Romans 14:1,13,19-20,22 MSG).

Epieikeia

"Let your gentle spirit [*epieikeia*] be known to all men" (Philippians 4:5). The Greek word *epieikeia* is difficult to translate.

Various translators render it "forbearing spirit," "gentleness," "unselfish," "considerate," "moderation," "patience" and "magnanimity." It is believed to refer to one who doesn't take extreme stands, someone who is sweet, soft-spirited, reasonable, lenient, overlooks faults and failures of others, and is willing to yield personal rights. This is the person's attitude toward Christians, the unsaved, and even persecutors. The Greeks explained the word this way: "justice and something better than justice."[8] They held that a man had *epieikeia* when he knew when to apply the strict letter of the law and when to show compassion. Christ showed *epieikeia* to the woman taken in adultery. The individual whose life is transformed by God from the inside out will show *epieikeia*. Another way to say it is "be Christ-like."

The Difference Between Law and Grace

I once heard a story of a woman married to a demanding husband. He would give her a list of the things she was to do each day, and then at night he would check on her diligence. She complied to the best of her ability; nevertheless, she never could please him. They lived with constant tension despite her best attempts at fulfilling his dictates. Eventually he died, and she married a man who deeply loved her and she him. One day she was cleaning some old drawers and ran across a list of duties that her first husband had given. She was astonished to discover that she was fulfilling all the demands of her first husband, but now she was acting from an overflow of a loving relationship, not out of duty.

Discussion Questions

1. Share your spiritual journey chart from last week with the group.

2. How do you know if you are living out of the flesh or out of faith?

3. Does the author make too big a deal out of the motive behind obedience? Isn't the important thing that we are obedient?

4. What is the relationship between being a "successful Christian" and a life of faith and adoration?

5. How would it affect our presentation of the gospel if we owned our brokenness before the church and unbelieving world?

6. Do you think the power that sin has over us will greatly change depending on the stage of growth in which we are living?

7. How transparent can you be with those around you? What hinders you from being more transparent?

Experiencing God's Love and Grace This Week

During the next week, rather than focusing on what you do for God, focus on the fact that you, as a branch, are connected to Christ, the vine. Visualize his dwelling within you, flowing through you, and working through you (see John 15:1-16). Be more aware of the promptings of the Holy Spirit in your life. Meditate on Galatians 5:6,13,16,18,22-23, and Romans 1:4-5; 16:25-26. Consider marking them in your Bible and memorizing some of them.

16

Don't Travel Without
a Roadmap

As we scan the horizon through the ages, we easily see crises and stages of growth in the lives of saints. Some of the turning points in the spiritual journeys of prominent Christians have become legendary: Francis of Assisi's renunciation of his family's wealth; Martin Luther's agonized confessions and penance, his enlightening study of Romans, his Ninety-Five Theses posted on the Wittenberg church door; John Wesley's zealous early years, his difficult missionary endeavor, and the Aldersgate meeting at which he felt his heart "strangely warmed" and which forever changed his attitude and experience of the Lord. Fanny Crosby is an example of many who, despite tremendous handicaps, lived a life glorifying to God. In her situation a quack doctor caused her to become blind at six weeks of age, yet she went on to serve the poor and needy and to write more than 8,000 hymns with a most joyful spirit. The list could go on and on. Let's take a look at the lives of some of the saints, both old and new, and see what directions they might give us for our spiritual journey.

Spiritual Growth Throughout Christian History

One can see stages of growth in virtually all of the Old Testament figures. For example, Moses grew up in the courts of

Pharaoh and was an "arrogant, self-willed man" the first 40 years of his life. Then he became a fugitive because of murder and spent the next 40 years as a shepherd and a "broken man" in the wilderness.[1] These were the crises and stages he went through in preparation for his eventual position of leadership at 80 years of age!

Perhaps the most vivid scriptural example of stages of growth is the apostle Paul. He undoubtedly made a decision to serve God as a young boy, and he is the epitome of someone who works exceedingly hard at "knowing and doing" everything humanly possible to please God. He had the right pedigree, impeccably kept the Jewish traditions and Law, and set himself up as an expert on God's truth. In fact, he was a zealot: He not only determined if a person was following God's truth, but he executed judgment, up to and including murder, on the person who wasn't following God's truth…according to Paul. But Paul was stuck striving to *earn* God's favor (Philippians 3:4-6).

With the revelation of Christ on the Damascus Road, a remarkable change took place in Paul. Christ replaced the Torah—the Jewish Law—as the center of his life. But God wasn't through with him. Paul spent the next three years alone in the desert of Arabia, after which he became an itinerant preacher. Apparently the early years weren't that successful until he began to minister under the leadership of Barnabas. It was on his missionary journeys where he grew to become the apostle that we know.[2] Only then did Paul start to see the marvelous truths of the life in Christ. Galatians 2:20 became his hallmark: "I have been crucified with Christ; and it is no longer I who live, but Christ lives in me; and the life which I now live in the flesh I live by faith in the Son of God, who loved me and gave Himself up for me." In the book of Philippians, Paul stated that all his religious accomplishments that were once so important to him were now like the most putrefying waste he could imagine. He gave up all of his self-effort so that he would "be found in him, not having [his] own righteousness, which is of the law, but that which is through the faith of Christ, the righteousness which is of God by faith" (Philippians 3:9 KJV).

Postbiblical saints who traveled through various stages of spiritual growth are also abundant. Marguerite Porete and St. Teresa of Avila of the thirteenth and sixteenth centuries had deep, experiential relationships with God that, frankly, challenge me. They clearly saw the Christian life as a journey. Marguerite wrote about seven stages of growth and St. Teresa used the analogy of a castle with rooms through which we must travel as we grow in our spiritual life. Their walk with God and dedication to Christ was unquestionable. Marguerite Porete was unwilling to capitulate to the spiritual mores of the time that violated her conscience so she was burned at the stake by the religious leaders of the day.

John Bunyan, who lived in the mid-seventeenth century, was a disturbed youth given to profanity before accepting Christ. Accounts suggest that for a time he was stuck as a "Believing Doubter." Even as a preacher he didn't experience freedom initially. He says, "I preached....I went myself in chains, to preach to them in chains." Then suddenly he came to an awareness that "my righteousness was Jesus Christ himself," and he learned "the wonderful reality of 'the life that is Christ.'" This love and mercy started to overflow in his life. "Then his preaching took on more of an exaltation of 'Jesus Christ'... [and] he began to teach 'the mystery of the union of Christ.'"[3] Though in prison, he wrote his profound bestseller *Pilgrim's Progress,* which depicts an individual's stages of growth.

A contemporary of John Bunyan, though they probably never met, was the monk Brother Lawrence, who discovered what it meant to "practice the presence of God." He strongly influenced Hudson Taylor, and these two men have been the inspiration for many to move beyond the drudgery of trying to earn God's pleasure to joy in experiencing the "exchanged life." Since I have discussed these individuals in previous chapters, let's turn our attention to others who clearly were influenced by them.

Andrew Murray, of South Africa, was born in the latter part of the nineteenth century. He pastored several South African churches, helped found two institutions of higher learning, was president of the YMCA, and strongly promoted missions. He is known for his life of prayer, preaching, and his inspirational writing that had a profound influence on many throughout the next century.[4] He describes several "stages" in his Christian life: There was a "lower stage," a period of ten years in which he appeared to be zealous and happy in his work as a minister, yet he experienced dissatisfaction, restlessness, lack of power, struggling. He said, "Everything troubled me." He went on to say:

> Later on, my mind became much exercised about the baptism of the Holy Spirit.…Through all these stumblings God led me, without any very special experience that I can point to; but as I look back I do believe now that He was giving me more and more of His blessed Spirit, had I but known it better.…
>
> I can help you more, perhaps, by speaking, not of any marked experience, but by telling very simply what I think God has given me now, in contrast to the first ten years of my Christian life. In the first place, I have learnt to place myself before God every day, as a vessel to be filled with His Holy Spirit. He has filled me with the blessed assurance that He, as the everlasting God, has guaranteed His work in me. If there is one lesson that I am learning day by day, it is this: that it is God who worketh all in all.[5]

Andrew Murray learned how to "abide in the Vine, by implicit obedience," and his desire was to be known "simply as a follower of Jesus."[6]

Charles G. Trumbull was a prominent evangelical leader and editor of the *Sunday School Times*. He was chairman of the Council of the Victorious Life Testimony and one of the founders of America's Keswick, a center known as a place where God speaks to hearts.[7] He accepted Christ at 15 and immediately gave himself to God's work. Despite strenuous efforts, he felt he was a failure, struggling with "besetting sins" and living at "lower levels" with spiritual barrenness going "down in the depths of defeat." This went on for some *20 years*.[8] All these years he was seeking more, when he met some men who were conspicuously blessed in their Christian service and seemed to have a *consciousness of Christ* that he did not have.[9]

Through their influence and prayer, he sought the Lord, and a new conception of Christ encompassed him. He became aware that the major resource in the Christian was Jesus Christ—period. An epiphany experience occurred as he became conscious of *Christ being in him* and *Christ being his very life*. In the past he had supposed that "to me to live is to be Christ-like" or "to me to live is to have Christ's help" or "to me to live is to serve Christ." He now became aware of what "to me to live is Christ" really meant—the awareness that the fullness of Christ was actually residing in him, and his living was in the strength of Christ.

Trumbull elaborates on his dramatic experience in *The Life that Wins* by telling how he learned that his greatest spiritual asset was a habitual consciousness of the presence of Jesus in his life, and that whenever his mind was free of other obligations, it would naturally turn to focus on Christ. Christ became a friend to him, with whom he would remain in dialog throughout the day.[10]

Charles Trumbull's life was radically changed, and he saw God's hand of blessing on his life and ministry. Others said that he was buoyant and joyous. "So dynamic and satisfying was the transformation that came to Dr. Trumbull by the indwelling Saviour that everywhere, by life, word, and pen, he gave testimony to *the life that is Christ.*"[11]

Ian Thomas was a major in the British Army during World War II. His Christian life was characterized by ceaseless activity, but he saw no conversions. He felt deep discouragement. He was barren, empty, and exhausted. "Most folk break down simply because they are carrying all their own burdens and all their own problems, sleeping with them crowding in on their minds; nervous strain comes from assuming a responsibility for things that [were] never intended to be carried by you," he observed. After struggling for seven years trying to live for Christ, he cried out to God in prayer and became aware that the answer was not his trying to live the Christian life, but *allowing Christ to live through him.* He felt liberated. He didn't need a new method or technique, but *Christ's life in him.* He described it as "Christ-activity." He became aware that "you cannot have *My* life and *your* program. You can only have *My* life for *My* program!" After this revelation his life became both an adventure and productive.[12] He went on to develop a worldwide ministry that included conference centers around the world: he was founder and general director of Capernwray Missionary Fellowship of Torchbearers.[13]

Catherine Marshall, a pastor's daughter and the wife of Peter Marshall, a former chaplain of the U.S. Senate, clearly depicts stages of growth in her journey of faith. She says, "The search for God begins at the point of need" and when about ten years old she went forward to the invitation of her preacher-father at the end of a church service. She became a preacher's wife, speaking and leading Bible studies, but states that it was on an "organizational level." Then she became aware of the need to make Christ the ruler of her life and have a "vital experience" with God—but how? Soon after her serene life was interrupted with the dreaded disease tuberculosis, for which there was no good treatment at the time. In the midst of her despair she discovered "the prayer of relinquishment"—yielding to God the residual things she was holding onto. In the process, she learned how to have an experiential relationship with Christ. Later she discovered the person of the Holy Spirit, the Helper, Teacher, Comforter, and Counselor. She says "nothing dramatic happened to me—no rushing wind or ecstasy" but she entered into a new joy sensing his presence in her. She found that the Holy Spirit repeatedly brings one back to an emphasis on Jesus in one's life and a sense of his Presence. Through Catherine Marshall's speaking and books thousands have been led to experience God in a new, deeper and exciting way.[14]

This extremely brief recital conveys how a few great men and women of God went through various stages in their Christian growth and gives us some direction and a roadmap for our lives.

A Unique Journey

Everyone's journey is unique. Think of Abraham, Joseph, David, Peter, and Paul. How different their journeys were! It's been said, "Don't make a principle out of your experience; let God be as original with others as He was with you."[15] We must be careful that we don't expect or demand that we follow exactly the same path as some admired saint or that we place such expectations on others.

Recently I was asked to lead a small group using assigned material that was not where my head or heart was. The material was valid, good teaching, but very basic material that didn't nurture or stimulate me—but it did stir others. That's an important lesson. Many of us are at dissimilar places in our walk with God, and thus the proper directions for other people might be very different than the course we need to take.

Similarities in Our Journey

On the other hand, there are many similarities in our journeys to be a people after God's own heart. James Gilchrist Lawson, who wrote almost a 100 years ago, and Dr. V. Raymond Edman, a more recent writer, detail the experiences of outstanding Christians. They were all different, yet patterns emerge and a wonderful harmony is revealed in their lives.[16] So what are some of the common ingredients that repeatedly emerge as we study the lives of those who have gone before us and experienced the abundant life?

Awareness of Need

We don't seek water until we are aware that we are thirsty. John 7:37 says, "If anyone is thirsty, let him come to Me and drink." A common starting point, whether we are "saved" or not, is to have a deep hunger for God. Actually, I believe we all have that hunger, that "God-shaped vacuum"; unfortunately, Satan has distracted many of us with the things of this world in an attempt to quench that internal void. When the individual pursuing God becomes aware that the mirages of this world will not satisfy, he appropriately faces his own neediness and seeks the true source to satisfy that need—God.

Lordship and Centrality of Christ

Those before us who experienced the overflowing, abundant life made God in the person of Christ their most important pursuit in life. There lives weren't driven, but they were *intentional*. Christ was the Lord of their lives and their purpose for living (Romans 6:13; 12:1). As Paul said, "For to me, to live is Christ" (Philippians 1:21). Furthermore, the notable Christians had a conscious realization of Christ's abiding presence—that Christ actually dwelt in them (Galatians 2:20; Colossians 1:26-27). A.W. Tozer said it so well:

> True Christian experience must always include a genuine encounter with God....The spiritual giants of old were men who at some time became acutely conscious of the real Presence of God and maintained that consciousness for the rest of their lives....*They experienced God*....They walked in conscious communion with the real Presence and addressed their prayers to God with the...conviction that they were addressing Someone actually there.[17]

Appreciation of the Vital Role of The Holy Spirit

Christ says, "It is to your advantage that I go away" so that "He, the Spirit of truth" will come and guide us, being our comforter and helper (see John 15:26–16:14). If we are going to have a vital Christian life, it is essential that we deeply value the person of the Holy Spirit and the important role he plays in our lives.

Some individuals will have a special manifestation of the Holy Spirit. Many saints in history actually sought an experience of the fullness of the Holy Spirit. Others, though not seeking any special encounter with the Holy Spirit, in fact, had such. Some testify of a significant increase in productiveness for the kingdom after such an encounter. But whether or not one has such an experience, it is crucial that we acknowledge the important place of the Holy Spirit in our lives. I do not believe, however, that we should demand of ourselves or others that they or we have any special manifestation of the Holy Spirit. Likewise, we should never minimize the experience of another person. Remember, we are all different and the Holy Spirit chooses to work differently in various people: "But one and the same Spirit works all these things, distributing to each one individually just as He wills" (1 Corinthians 12:11).

Proper Importance of the Bible

God's most definitive message to humanity is the Word of God—the Bible. It's God's authentic word and the standard of all Christian faith and conduct. It is our means of spiritual nourishment. Its *aim* is to bring us to a living, vibrant, experiential relationship with Christ.

A Life of Faith

Implied in each of the points just mentioned is that this entire life in Christ is a life of faith—the kind of faith that gets in the wheelbarrow (see chapter 13). For truly "without faith it is impossible to please Him" (Hebrews 11:6).

Keeping the Focus Right

Dr. Roy Hession was a British evangelist who had a wide ministry under the sponsorship of Worldwide Evangelization Crusade. Some years ago I read my wife's copy of his outstanding book *The Calvary Road*, which emphasized "dying to self."[18] Then 8 years later, seemingly as a new step or stage in the author's growth he and his wife published *We Would See Jesus*, where they "learned" that they didn't need to focus on the negative but rather on the positive of looking unto Jesus.[19] Some 17 years after their first publication, Roy published *Be Filled Now*, where the emphasis is on allowing the Holy Spirit to lead us.[20] Sometimes when I go by bookracks I will see *The Calvary Road* and not the other books. In fact, *The Calvary Road* sells almost 4 times as many books as *We Would See Jesus* and over 35 times more than *Be Filled Now*.[21] It seems that people prefer to teach and concentrate on crucifying the self rather than focusing on Jesus and being filled by His blessed Spirit. We need to fix our gaze on Jesus, allowing his Spirit to fill us. When we do that, self will appropriately get out of the way!

Rivers of Living Water

As we read the accounts of the great men and women of God, we see that their journeys often took them from thirsting after God and righteousness to a place of being satiated with the living water (John 7:37-39). Sure, they still struggled with illness, discouragement, and trials, but in general, after some discovery of the life of faith and the presence of Christ in their lives, their lives were characterized more by abundant life.

My prayer for you is that you will allow the Holy Spirit full access to your heart. He will enlighten you to understand and internalize Christ's phenomenal love for you (Ephesians 1–3). I also pray that if you should be stuck someplace along the way, that you will take the next step of faith so you can taste what God has desired for you—that you would personally experience the living presence of Christ in you.

Discussion Questions

1. As you consider this book and the discussions that have followed each chapter, what has impacted your life the most?

2. Was there a particular topic or chapter you found difficult? Why?

3. What role does the Holy Spirit play in your life? Has that changed?

4. Which Christian throughout history do you most admire? Which living saint has influenced your life the most?

5. Can you focus too much on your spiritual growth and miss Jesus?

6. Why do you think some people are prone to focus on "dying to self" rather than focusing on Jesus? What are the results of such a focus?

7. How can you experience a greater transformation of your life into the image of Christ?

Experiencing God's Love and Grace for the Rest of Your Life

Prayerfully consider what truths the Holy Spirit has been impressing upon you as you have read this book and discussed it with others. How might you better assimilate these truths into the rest of your life? If you would like to read in greater depth about lives that have been transformed, I encourage you to read V. Raymond Edman's *They Found the Secret: Twenty Transformed Lives That Reveal a Touch of Eternity*.[22]

The Journey Ahead

We are all "works in process," trying to capture the essence of a life transformed by Christ. There is a lot of good material and programs available on Evangelization (Stage 1) and the To Know/To Do (Stage 2) stages of growth. These are the focus of most of our discipleship programs—and for the most part, they are doing a pretty good job. These first two stages are easier to teach, and they lend themselves to a more structured approach. But herein lay some potential problems. We need to: (1) keep in mind that our primary aim is to grow in our relationship with Christ; (2) carefully watch that legalism doesn't creep in; and (3) guard that our activities don't keep people from the more ambiguous and difficult tasks of the later stages of spiritual growth. Working on the outside is a lot easier than working on the inside of our lives, but inside is where *all* spiritual transformation takes place.

Furthermore, Stage 2 is controllable, predictable, can be addictive, and even lends itself to building monuments to ourselves. It can be scary to move beyond its "safe" boundaries. In fact, congregations that focus primarily on Stage 2 will face considerable resistance to change, whether the pastoral staff or laity fosters it.

We need to be open to the possibility that individuals *and* churches can become stuck in their spiritual journeys.

As we go to higher levels of spiritual transformation, the primary method of teaching is by dependence on the *Holy Spirit, modeling,* and *inspiration.* For the most part this is "caught" and not taught. That is why it is extremely difficult to package it into a formula. It is also hard for transformation to germinate in a church unless it begins at the "top." If this were to take place, there may be some radical changes in how we often "do church." I know of churches, denominations, and seminaries that are establishing structures to promote an emphasis on spiritual formation—and I think that is great. We need such an emphasis. There are tools available and now being promoted to assist us in growing deeper in our spiritual lives. Some people and studies are going back to the early leaders of the church for examples and spiritual disciplines.

Additional resources are some tremendous seminars and conferences that address this issue of transformation and spiritual growth. In some of these I see the potential of two trends: One is to make growth totally of grace, without any articulation of our roles or responsibilities. The other trend—the American way—is to figure out methods to package and promote growth. Both perspectives have truth in them, but there is also a down side. The aim of transforming our inner beings into the image of Christ can get lost because this can't be put into a formula and packaged. It is literally a walk of faith. I believe the most effective means for promoting spiritual transformation will be through modeling, emphasizing relationships over strategies, and accepting each other's differences.

We need to carefully keep our primary focus on Christ, who is walking on the path with us—and is, in fact, *in* us. Christ's challenge is, "Come, follow me," and "when He, the Spirit of truth, comes, He will guide you into all the truth" (Luke 9:23; John 16:13). The only certified, guaranteed program of spiritual transformation is Jesus Christ.

Bibliography

Numerous resources are available on the subjects covered in this book. On specific topics, see the notes. The following is a list of the books I strongly recommend. That does not mean I endorse every teaching in a book, but I commend the vast majority of it and believe the book is well worth your time.

Benner, David G. *Surrender to Love*. Downers Grove, IL: InterVarsity Press, 2003. This is an excellent book focusing on our need to surrender to God to experience his love.

Curtis, Brent, and John Eldredge. *The Sacred Romance: Drawing Closer to the Heart of God*. Nashville: Thomas Nelson Publishers, 1997. This book is very illuminating regarding our love relationship with Christ.

Dearborn, Tim. *Taste & See: Awakening Our Spiritual Senses*. Downers Grove, IL: InterVarsity Press, 1996. The primary emphasis is that God wants us to know him through Christ.

Edman, V. Raymond. *They Found the Secret: Twenty Transformed Lives That Reveal a Touch of Eternity*. Grand Rapids, MI: Zondervan Publishing House, 1972. This is an excellent book on 20 saints who have much to teach us.

Foster, Richard J. *Celebration of Discipline*. New York: HarperCollins Publishers, 1998. This is a classic on spiritual disciplines.

Hagberg, Janet O., and Robert A. Guelich. *The Critical Journey: Stages in the Life of Faith*. Salem, WI: Sheffield Publishing Company, 1995. I did not discover this book until after I had completed a semifinal draft of this book. I was amazed at the number of similarities in our books. I would strongly recommend this book, provided you don't get hung up on their somewhat broader view of justification.

Issler, Klaus. *Wasting Time with God*. Downers Grove, IL: InterVarsity Press, 2001. An excellent book on spirituality and friendship with God.

Kelly, Thomas R. *A Testament of Devotion.* New York: Harper Collins Publishing, 1996. The content of this book touched the depths of my heart.

Brother Lawrence. *The Practice of the Presence of God.* Old Tappan, NJ: Whitaker House, 1982. This is a classic little book about focusing our minds on the Lord throughout the day.

Lawson, James Gilchrist. *Deeper Experiences of Famous Christians.* Anderson, IN: Whitaker House, 1998. An older book, somewhat harder reading, nevertheless contains excellent information.

McVey, Steve. *Grace Walk: What You've Always Wanted in the Christian Life.* Eugene, OR: Harvest House Publishers, 1995. This is an excellent book on grace.

Nee, Watchman. *The Normal Christian Life.* Wheaton, IL: Tyndale House Publishers, 1977. This is a good book on the exchanged life but somewhat hard to read. Some Christians have trouble with some of Watchman Nee's material.

Ortberg, John. *The Life You've Always Wanted.* Grand Rapids, MI: Zondervan, 2002. Basic but excellent.

Tan, Siang-Yang. *Rest: Experiencing God's Peace in a Restless World.* Ann Arbor, MI: Servant Publications, 2000. This is a good book on experiencing God's rest.

Taylor, Howard, and Geraldine Taylor. *Hudson Taylor's Spiritual Secret.* Chicago: Moody Publishers, 1987. This is an excellent book on this missionary's life. One chapter seems to be the original material that has influenced so many on the exchanged life.

Thrall, Bill, Bruce McNicol, and John Lynch. *TrueFaced.* Colorado Springs: NavPress, 2003. This is an excellent book and among the easier ones to read. I especially liked chapter 5, which is worth the price of the book. It contrasts the emphasis of pleasing God versus trusting God.

Tozer, A.W. *The Pursuit of God.* Harrisburg, PA: Christian Publications, Inc, 1997. Tozer has many paperback books that remain in print a half-century after first published. Frankly, I like Tozer and have been inspired by many of his books.

Trumball, Charles G. *The Life That Wins.* This is an address given by Charles Trumbull in 1911. This is public-domain material, about five pages in length, and can be downloaded from several sites including: http://www.cdlf.org/ftp/ or http://www.bereanpublishers.co.nz/ Testimonies/ Charles_Trumbull_Testimony.htm. This is excellent on the concept that Christ is in you.

Wilkins, Michael J. *In His Image.* Colorado Springs: NavPress, 1997. Good, basic information on whether or not it really is possible to become like Jesus.

Willard, Dallas. *Renovation of the Heart.* Colorado Spring: NavPress, 2002. An outstanding book but somewhat hard to read. However, reading some of Willard's books is a must for any serious follower of Christ.

_____. *The Divine Conspiracy.* New York: HarperSanFrancisco, 1998. This is a classic book named by *Christianity Today* in 1999 as the one book you should read if you only read one book that year. It isn't easy reading, though it is more than worth the effort.

Notes

Stalled on the Journey

1. "Barna Continues to Defend Survey Showing Divorce Rates Among Christians," *Christian News Service*, http://www.worthynews.com/news -features/christian-divorce-rate.html.

2. "The Sex Lives of Christian Teens," *Today's Christian*, http://www. christianitytoday.com/tc/2003/002/7.28.html.

3. I am indebted to Ed Lassiter for this paragraph.

4. As reported in *Australian Christian Channel*, "Barna Sees Challenges Ahead for Churches to Remain Significant in Peoples Lives," http:/www.acctv.com. au/articledetail.asp?id=3535.

5. All illustrations in the book are true, however, in many instances pseudonyms are used and incidental facts altered to protect the identities of the individuals. Often stories are a composite of several individuals.

6. The first to write on stages of growth was the theologian Origen of Alexandria, who wrote in the third century. The best-known contemporary writer is James W. Fowler. Other individuals writing on the subject have 2, 3, 4, 6, 7, and 8 stages of growth. They include: Saint Bonaventura, Teresa of Avila, Augustine, Aelred of Rievaulx, Julian of Norwich, John of the Cross, Francis of Assisi, Marguerite Porete, Ignatius Loyola, John Bunyan, Sóren Kierkegaard, Evelyn Underhill, Elizabeth O'Connor, M. Scott Peck, "Search Institute," Janet Hagberg, and Robert Guelich.

Chapter 1—The Dutiful Christian

1. *Webster's College Dictionary* (New York: Random House, 1995), s.v. "driven."

2. Additional Scriptures include 1 Kings 3:10; Psalm 104:34; Proverbs 16:7; Jeremiah 6:20; 27:4-5; Malachi 3:3-4; Matthew 3:17; John 8:29; 1 Thessalonians 2:4; 4:1-2; Hebrews 11:5-6; 13:20-21; and 1 John 3:21-23.

3. John Ortberg, *The Life You've Always Wanted* (Grand Rapids, MI: Zondervan, 2002), p. 39.

4. Steve McVey, *Grace Walk: What You've Always Wanted in the Christian Life* (Eugene, OR: Harvest House Publishers, 1995), p. 80.

5. Bill Thrall, Bruce McNicol, and John Lynch, *TrueFaced* (Colorado Springs: NavPress, 2003), p. 89.

6. Dr. William Gaultiere, *Returning to the Father* (Chicago: Moody Press, 1993), pp. 80-81, 92.

7. Dallas Willard, "Spiritual Disciplines, Spiritual Formation, and the Restoration of the Soul," *Journal of Psychology and Theology* 26, no. 1 (1998): 107.

8. Thrall, McNicol, Lynch, *TrueFaced*.

Chapter 2—The Corporate Christian

1. I am not sure where the term "group think" originated, but you can find numerous references on the Web. In the secular sphere it generally refers to pressure to conform, self-censorship, an illusion of unanimity, and so forth.

2. Michael J. Wilkins, *In His Image* (Colorado Springs: NavPress, 1997), pp. 53-54.

3. Janet O. Hagberg and Robert A. Guelich, *The Critical Journey: Stages in the Life of Faith* (Salem, WI: Sheffield Publishing Company, 1995), p. 82.

4. Wilkins, *In His Image*, p. 176.

5. David G. Benner, *Surrender to Love* (Downers Grove, IL: InterVarsity Press, 2003), p. 56.

6. Eugene H. Peterson, *The Wisdom of Each Other: A Conversation Between Spiritual Friends* (Grand Rapids, MI: Zondervan, 1998), p. 24.

7. Brent Curtis and John Eldredge, *The Sacred Romance: Drawing Closer to the Heart of God* (Nashville: Thomas Nelson, 1997), pp. 169-70.

8. Henri Nouwen, *The Way of the Heart* (New York: Ballantine, 1981), pp. 46-47.

9. John Eldredge, *Waking the Dead* (Nashville: Thomas Nelson, 2003), p. 218.

10. Steve McVey, *Living in the Kingdom of God Where Grace Rules* (Eugene, OR: Harvest House Publishers, 1998), p. 145.

11. Roy and Revel Hession, *We Would See Jesus* (Fort Washington, PA: Christian Literature Crusade, 1958), pp. 14-15.

Chapter 3—The Expert Christian

1. Quoted in Brent Curtis and John Eldredge, *The Sacred Romance: Drawing Closer to the Heart of God* (Nashville: Thomas Nelson, 1997), p. 45.

2. The five points of Calvinism actually don't come from Calvin himself but from the Synod of Dort about 60 years after Calvin.

3. As quoted in A.W. Tozer, *That Incredible Christian* (Harrisburg, PA: Christian Publications, 1964), p. 59.

4. A.W. Tozer, *The Root of the Righteous* (Harrisburg, PA: Christian Publications, 1955), p. 68.

5. William Barclay, *The Letters to the Philippians, Colossians, and Thessalonians* (Louisville, KY: Westminster John Knox, 1975), p. 31.

6. According to *Newsweek*, April 16, 2001, p. 49, as recorded in Dallas Willard, *Renovation of the Heart* (Colorado Springs: NavPress, 2002), pp. 22, 258.

7. William Byron Forbush, ed., *Fox's Book of Martyrs* (Philadelphia: The John C. Winston Company, 1926), pp. 185-88.

8. Klaus Issler, *Wasting Time with God* (Downers Grove, IL: InterVarsity Press, 2001), pp. 74-75.

9. Willard, *Renovation of the Heart*, pp. 237-38.

10. A. W. Tozer, *The Pursuit of God* (Harrisburg, PA: Christian Publications, Inc, 1948), pp. 9-10.

11. Tozer, *The Root of the Righteous*, pp. 77-79.

12. Issler, *Wasting Time*, pp. 155-56.

13. Warren W. Wiersbe, *Be Joyful* (Colorado Springs: Chariot Victor, 1974), p. 43.

14. Tozer, *Root of the Righteous*, p. 34.

Chapter 4—The Grace-Abuser Christian

1. I am quoting from a book of a well-respected Christian leader, but choose to not give the source as my aim is not to criticize him personally but only an idea he is promoting. In fact, I agree with most of what he says.

2. I am quoting from a book of a well-respected Christian leader. I'm not giving the source because my aim is not to criticize him personally but only an idea he is promoting. In fact, I agree with most of what he says.

3. A.W. Tozer, *Of God and Men* (Harrisburg, PA: Christian Publications, 1960), p. 49.

4. John Piper, *Future Grace* (Sisters, OR: Multnomah Press, 1995), p. 364; verses that follow this quote include 1 Corinthians 3:8; Ephesians 6:8; 1 Thessalonians 1:3; 2 Thessalonians 1:11; Lk 19:12-27, and the parable of the talents.

5. Robert Farrar Capon, *The Mystery of Christ...And Why We Don't Get It* (Grand Rapids, MI: Eerdmans, 1993), pp. 27, 115, 117.

6. Piper, *Future Grace* (Sisters, OR: Multnomah Press, 1995), pp. 11-12.

Chapter 5—The Resistant Christian

1. A.W. Tozer, *The Root of the Righteous* (Harrisburg, PA: Christian Publications, 1955), pp. 129-30.

2. See Matthew 26:38 NKJV and 2 Corinthians 6:10.

3. W. Phillip Keller, *A Common Man's Quest for God: Wonder o' the Wind* (Waco, TX: Word Books, 1982), pp. 148-49.

Chapter 6—The Emotional Christian

1. *Webster's College Dictionary* (New York: Random House, 1995), s.v. "mystic."

2. Madeleine S. Miller and J. Lane Miller, *Harper's Bible Dictionary* (New York: Harper & Row, 1961), s.v. "mystic."

3. James Emery White, *Embracing the Mysterious God: Loving the God We Don't Understand* (Downers Grove, IL: InterVarsity Press, 2003); see also: Hebrews 11:1: Isaiah 55:9; Ephesians 5:32.

4. C.S. Lewis, *Mere Christianity* (London: Collins Press, 1952), p. 156.

5. As described in Elizabeth O'Connor, *Journey Inward, Journey Outward* (New York: Harper & Row, 1968), p. 112.

Chapter 7—The Runt Christian

1. John Piper, *Desiring God* (Sisters, OR: Multnomah Press, 1996), p. 54.

2. John Piper, *Future Grace* (Sisters, OR: Multnomah Press, 1995), p. 249.

3. Janet O. Hagberg and Robert A. Guelich, *The Critical Journey: Stages in the Life of Faith* (Salem, WI: Sheffield Publishing Co., 1995), pp. 63-64.

4. A.W. Tozer, *The Root of the Righteous* (Harrisburg, PA: Christian Publications, 1955), p. 112.

Chapter 8—Getting the Right Start

1. Viggo B. Olsen with Jeanette Lockebie, *Daktar/Diplomat in Bangladesh* (Chicago: Moody Press, 1973).

2. See Mark 1:15; Luke 13:3; Acts 3:19; Romans 3:23; 6:23.

3. See John 3:16; Ephesians 2:8-9.

4. See James 2:19; Romans 5:8; John 14:6, 1:12; Revelation 3:20; John 5:24; 1 John 5:11-12.

5. For more information along this line see Dwight L. Carlson, *Why Do Christians Shoot Their Wounded? Helping (Not Hurting) Those with Emotional Difficulties* (Downers Grove, IL: InterVarsity Press, 1994).

Chapter 9—Knowing and Doing

1. See Revelation 1:3; Acts 17:11; Psalm 1:2-3; 119:9-11; 1 Timothy 4:13-15.

Chapter 10—The Authentic Heart

1. There are so many excellent verses on God's looking at our hearts and motives. A few such verses are: 1 Chronicles 28:9; 29:17; Ecclesiastes 12:14; Proverbs 20:27; Revelation 2:23.

2. See Hebrews 11 and Genesis 12–23.

Chapter 11—Experiencing God

1. A.W. Tozer, *The Pursuit of God* (Harrisburg, PA: Christian Publications, 1948), p. 13.

2. Brent Curtis and John Eldredge, *The Sacred Romance: Drawing Closer to the Heart of God* (Nashville: Thomas Nelson, 1997), p. 82.

3. Rick Warren, *The Purpose-Driven Life* (Grand Rapids, MI: Zondervan, 2002), p. 64.

4. Tim Dearborn, *Taste & See: Awakening Our Spiritual Senses* (Downers Grove, IL: InterVarsity Press, 1996), p. 83.

5. J.I. Packer, *Knowing God* (Downers Grove, IL: InterVarsity Press, 1973), p. 35.

6. Ken Gire, *Windows of the Soul* (Grand Rapids, MI: Zondervan, 1996), p. 11.

7. Klaus Issler, *Wasting Time with God* (Downers Grove, IL: InterVarsity Press, 2001), pp. 16-17.

8. Tozer, *The Pursuit of God*, pp. 36-38.

9. Eugene H. Peterson, *Answering God: The Psalms as Tools for Prayer* (San Francisco: HarperSanFrancisco, 1989), p. 12.

10. Issler, *Wasting Time with God*, p. 252.

11. Brother Lawrence, *The Practice of the Presence of God* (Old Tappan, NJ: Spire Books, 1969), pp. 8, 12, 15, 18, 22.

12. A.W. Tozer, *That Incredible Christian* (Harrisburg, PA: Christian Publications, Inc., 1964), p. 137.

13. Richard A. Swenson, *Margin: How to Create the Emotional, Physical, Financial & Time Reserves You Need* (Colorado Springs: NavPress, 1992) and *A Minute of Margin: Restoring Balance to Busy Lives* (Colorado Springs: NavPress, 2003).

14. Dearborn, *Taste & See*, p. 62.

Chapter 12—The Crises of Faith

1. I describe this in greater detail in my book *Why Do Christians Shoot Their Wounded? Helping (Not Hurting) Those with Emotional Difficulties* (Downers Grove, IL: InterVarsity Press, 1994).

2. My daughter and I describe these events in detail in the book we coauthored: Dwight Carlson, M.D. and Susan Carlson Wood, *When Life Isn't Fair: Why We Suffer and How God Heals* (Eugene, OR: Harvest House Publishers, 1989).

3. Quoted in Steve McVey, *Grace Walk: What You've Always Wanted in the Christian Life* (Eugene, OR: Harvest House Publishers, 1995), p. 9.

4. Dr. and Mrs. Howard Taylor, *Hudson Taylor's Spiritual Secret* (Chicago: Moody Press, 1932), p. 182.

5. Bill Thrall, Bruce McNicol, and John Lynch, *TrueFaced* (Colorado Springs: NavPress, 2003), p. 197.

6. Richard J. Foster and Emilie Griffin, eds., *Spiritual Classics* (New York: HarperSanFrancisco, 2000), pp. 22-25.

7. M. Scott Peck, *The Different Drum: Community Making and Peace* (New York: Simon & Schuster, 1987), p. 188.

8. Janet O. Hagberg and Robert A. Guelich, *The Critical Journey: Stages in the Life of Faith* (Salem, WI: Sheffield Publishing Company, 1995). pp. 93-94.

9. Gordon MacDonald, "Knockouts," *Conversations* 1, no. 2 (Fall 2003): 16-19.

Chapter 13—The Exchanged Life

1. Dr. and Mrs. Howard Taylor, *Hudson Taylor's Spiritual Secret* (Chicago: Moody Press, 1932), pp. 154-61.

2. Ibid., p. 164.

3. John Eldredge, *Waking the Dead* (Nashville: Thomas Nelson, 2003), pp. 54, 76; see also Romans 7:17-18,20,22.

4. Jean Francois Gravelet, "The Great Blondin," crossed the Niagara Gorge on a tightrope in 1859, <www.niagaraparks.com/aboutus/trivia.php>. Incidentally, he also crossed the Gorge with his hands manacled, and he crossed carrying his manager, Harry Colcord, on his back. They barely survived.

5. James W. Fowler, *Stages of Faith* (New York: HarperCollins, 1995), p. 16.

6. A.W. Tozer, *The Pursuit of God* (Harrisburg, PA: Christian Publications, 1948), p. 91.

7. This is a modification and restatement from Dallas Willard, *The Spirit of the Disciplines* (San Francisco: Harper & Row, 1988), p. 68, and Tim Dearborn, *Taste & See: Awakening Our Spiritual Senses* (Downers Grove, IL: InterVarsity Press, 1996), pp. 56-57.

8. Ibid., pp. 66-68.

9. Watchman Nee, *The Normal Christian Life* (Wheaton IL: Tyndale House, 1957), pp. 105-06.

10. Ibid., pp. 11, 150.

Chapter 14—The Life of Adoration

1. Story as told in Dwight Carlson and Susan Carlson Wood, *When Life Isn't Fair: Why We Suffer and How God Heals* (Eugene, OR: Harvest House Publishers, 1989), pp. 89-90.

2. Brent Curtis and John Eldredge, *The Sacred Romance: Drawing Closer to the Heart of God* (Nashville: Thomas Nelson, 1997), pp. 97-98.

3. David G. Benner, *Surrender to Love* (Downers Grove, IL: InterVarsity Press, 2003), p. 26.

4. Ibid., p. 32.

5. C. Baxter Kruger, *Parable of the Dancing God* (Downers Grove, IL: InterVarsity Press, 2001), pp. 6-7.

6. *Webster's College Dictionary* (New York: Random House, 1995), s.v. "bask."

7. Philip Yancey, *Disappointment with God* (Grand Rapids, MI: Zondervan, 1988), p. 149.

8. Curtis and Eldredge, *The Sacred Romance.*

9. Benner, *Surrender to Love*, p. 64.

10. R. Kent Hughes, *Disciplines of a Godly Man* (Wheaton, IL: Crossway Books, 1991), p. 107.

11. Quoted in Davis Duggins, "The Worship Gap," *Moody,* March/April 1996, p. 34, citing Robert Webber, *Worship Old and New.*

12. A.W. Tozer, *Born after Midnight* (Harrisburg, PA: Christian Publications, 1959), pp. 125-26.

13. Hughes, *Disciplines of a Godly Man,* p. 107.

14. Duggins, "The Worship Gap," p. 28, citing Robert Webber, *Worship Old and New.*

15. *Webster's College Dictionary,* s.v. "worship."

16. www.reformed.org/documents.

17. Some references on the "Spiritual Disciplines" include Richard J. Foster, *Celebration of Discipline* (New York: HarperCollins Publishers, 1998) and Dallas Willard, *The Spirit of the Disciplines* (San Francisco: Harper & Row, Publishers, 1988).

18. Janet O. Hagberg and Robert A. Guelich, *The Critical Journey: Stages in the Life of Faith* (Salem, WI: Sheffield Publishing Company, 1995), pp. 8-9.

19. Curtis and Eldrige, *The Sacred Romance.*

Chapter 15—The Transformed Life

1. David G. Benner, *Surrender to Love* (Downers Grove, IL: InterVarsity Press, 2003), pp. 58-59.

2. Brennan Manning, *Ruthless Trust* (New York: HarperSanFrancisco, 2000), p. 122.

3. Dallas Willard, *Renovation of the Heart* (Colorado Springs: NavPress, 2002), pp. 72, 195.

4. Dwight L. Carlson, *Run and Not Be Weary* (Old Tappan, NJ: Revel, 1974).

5. Dwight L. Carlson, *Energize Your Life* (Ross-shire, Great Britain: Christian Focus, 2003).

6. Manning, *Ruthless Trust,* p. 61.

7. A.W. Tozer, *Born After Midnight* (Harrisburg, PA: Christian Publications, 1959), pp. 76, 79, emphasis added.

8. William Barclay, *The Letters to the Philippians, Colossians, and Thessalonians* (Louisville: Westminster John Knox Press, 1975), p. 75.

Chapter 16—Don't Travel Without a Roadmap

1. Gene Edwards, *A Tale of Three Kings: A Study in Brokenness* (Wheaton, IL: Tyndale House, 1992), p. 89.

2. See Acts 9:1-30; 11:22-26; 13:1-3; 15:36-41; Galatians 1:13-24.

3. Dr. V. Raymond Edman, *They Found the Secret: Twenty Transformed Lives That Reveal a Touch of Eternity* (Grand Rapids, MI: Zondervan, 1960), pp. 30-34.

4. Richard J. Foster and Emilie Griffin, eds., *Spiritual Classics* (San Francisco: HarperSanFrancisco, 2000), p. 271.

5. Edman, *They Found the Secret,* p. 96.

6. Ibid., pp. 94, 97.

7. www.cdlf.org/ftp/.

8. Edman, *They Found the Secret,* pp. 120-21.

9. Charles G. Trumbull, *The Life That Wins,* an address given by Charles Trumbull in 1911; public-domain edition, ed. Clyde C. Price Jr., available from Christian Digital Library Foundation Electronic texts: http://www.cdlf.org/ftp/ (June 1997); from a print-media booklet not claiming copyright published by Christian Literature Crusade, Fort Washington, PA 19034.

10. Trumbull, *The Life That Wins.*

11. Edman, *They Found the Secret,* p. 120.

12. Ibid., pp. 138-44.

13. www.praize.com/sermons/IanThomas/.

14. Catherine Marshall, *Beyond Ourselves* (New York: Avon Books, 1961), pp. 17, 48-50, 93-94, 237, 245; Catherine Marshall, *Something More: In Search of a Deeper Faith* (Carmel, NY: Guideposts Assoc. Inc., 1974), pp. 268-281; www.intouch.org; www.wvwc.edu; http://members.tripod.com.

15. I believe Oswald Chambers was the origin of this quote.

16. James Gilchrist Lawson, *Deeper Experiences of Famous Christians* (Anderson, IN: Warner Press, 1911); Edman, *They Found the Secret.*

17. A.W. Tozer, *The Divine Conquest* (Westwood, NJ: Revell, 1950), pp. 26-27.

18. Roy Hession, *The Calvary Road* (Philadelphia: Christian Literature Crusade, 1950), p. 13.

19. Roy and Revel Hession, *We Would See Jesus* (Fort Washington, PA: Christian Literature Crusade, 1959), p. 3.

20. Roy Hession, *Be Filled Now* (Fort Washington, PA: Christian Literature Crusade, 1967).

21. Personal communication with Charles Hurd of Christian Literature Crusade, August 15, 2005.

22. Edman, *They Found the Secret.*

Other books
by Dwight Carlson

Overcoming Hurts and Anger
Why Do Christians Shoot Their Wounded?
Energize Your Life
When Life Isn't Fair
From Guilt to Grace
The Will of the Shepherd
Run and Not Be Weary

Other Great Books
from Harvest House Publishers

The Remarkable Prayers of the Bible
Jim George

Pull back the curtain and witness for yourself the meaningful communion that took place between God and men and women who followed Him wholeheartedly. As you listen to their prayers, you'll discover exciting truths that will transform your prayer life, including God considers no issue too small for us to bring to Him, God is a deliverer who hears us anyplace at anytime, and God is always in control, even in life's unexpected turns.

The Healing Power of Forgiveness
Ray Pritchard

Why is forgiveness so difficult at times? Must we forgive when it's the other person's fault? How should we handle repeat offenses? Humanly speaking, forgiveness isn't possible. The secret to forgiving others is God's grace. He is the Supreme Forgiver. From Him, we can learn how to let go of the past...forgive our enemies...and be released from feelings of anger, bitterness, and hurt.

Come, and experience the healing power of forgiveness. And know the incredible freedom that comes with letting go of the past.

Sandpaper People
Getting Along with the Ones Who Rub You the Wrong Way
Mary Southerland

"God, why did You put these problem people in my life?" The unwanted intrusion of a nosy neighbor...the exasperating call from your least favorite co-worker...the latest mess-up by the relative who doesn't seem to want to change...If you've run out of ideas for handling your difficult relationships, perhaps it's time to try a fresh approach. Working from a toolbox full of anecdotes and humor, Mary Southerland presents action principles for relating to the abrasive people in your life, such as recognizing their worth, knowing when to confront, and refusing to walk away.

Chapter-by-chapter questions and applications will help you recognize your own sandpaper tendencies and see your sandpaper people for what they are: opportunities from God to grow—while being transformed in the process.

Quiet Times for Those Who Need Comfort
H. Norman Wright

Are you overwhelmed with sadness? Has time seemed to stop for you? Do you just want to ask God why? You're not alone. Millions of people struggle with these painful emotions after experiencing a significant loss. They become mired in a fog of hopelessness and lack a clear sense of direction on how to get back to daily living. Bestselling author and counselor Norm Wright uses his own journey through grief along with years of counseling experience to help you learn how to draw strength in times of weakness, find comfort when hope is gone, and experience God's boundless love.

In these insightful devotions, you will explore how to clarify your feelings of loss, establish a healthy outlook on the future, find strength in the arms of your heavenly Father, and much more. Thoughtful questions, soul-searching statements, and encouraging anecdotes will refresh and renew a spirit of hope in you and help you find peace.